DWELLER *on the* THRESHOLD

Rudolf Joseph Lorenz Steiner
February 27, 1861 – March 30, 1925

FROM THE WORKS OF DR. RUDOLF STEINER

DWELLER *on the* THRESHOLD

ENCOUNTERING THE LORD OF KARMA

Dr. Douglas J. Gabriel

Our Spirit, LLC
2024

OUR SPIRIT, LLC

P. O. Box 355
Northville, MI 48167

www.ourspirit.com
www.neoanthroposophy.com
www.gospelofsophia.com
www.eternalcurriculum.com

2024 Copyright © by Our Spirit, LLC

ISBN: 978-1-963709-09-4

Distorted, selfish thoughts add to the horribly grotesque nature of the evil thoughts recorded by the Guardian. Our cruel and uncompassionate feelings create a monster that is composed of each of the evil emotions we ever secretly, or overtly, felt towards others or our own self.

The mean and mindless deeds we have done manifest before our soul as collective karma that first must be resolved and rectified before we can look at the three fearful parts of the Guardian. These parts of the Guardian are the karmic ballast, the negative spiritual gravity, that holds us back from ascending into the spiritual world beyond the threshold 'door.' Upon seeing the truth of our own self-knowledge, we all fall back in horror and disgust at our lack of consciousness and our extreme selfishness. This self-knowledge will rip the soul asunder if a strong, selfless consciousness does not sit on the 'throne of love' in the individual's heart.

Every single thought, feeling, or deed is written into the 'Book of Life' which is called the Akashic Records by many spiritual scientists. Just like Santa Claus keeps his book of good and bad deeds throughout the year, so, too, the Guardian remembers and records everything.

In ancient Egypt, it was believed that the canine headed god Anubis (Anpu), known as 'the First of the Westerners,' weighed the heart (Ib) against a feather after death to see if the dead should advance into the spiritual world or not. For many Christians, Jesus Christ is now the Lord of Karma who judges the soul after death and determines whether they go to Heaven, Purgatory, or Hell. Essentially, every authentic tradition has a description of meeting the Guardian of the Threshold between the physical and spiritual worlds. Each description looks different on the surface, but they all have the same underlying elements—karma must be weighed before anyone can go into the spiritual world.

An aspirant seeking initiation into the mystery wisdom of the ancients attempts to cross the threshold consciously through transcendent meditation, spiritual practices, and initiation. Initiation is not for the faint-hearted, fearful, or lazy person. The preparations for initiation can be extremely demanding and complicated, and in the end, the aspirant may faint at the threshold and not be able to resolve the sins the Guardian displays before the quaking consciousness of the aspirant. Many try and fail. Sometimes, the aspirant may 'lose their mind' in the process of attempting to cross the threshold before they are ready. And, even if the aspirant makes it across the threshold, it doesn't mean they have the moral strength to remember what they experienced in the spiritual world while they were there. Only the selfless desire to gain wisdom for the sake of the welfare of 'all sentient beings' will keep the aspirant consciously awake in the spiritual world and help the aspirant remember the communion he had with the beings in that world.

A true visit to the spirit world will usually fire the will of the aspirant to return with inspiration that can be turned into moral deeds of love, created out of complete freedom. The aspirant will feel as though all of the good thinking, feeling, and willing he/she has done is offered as food to the spiritual beings (spiritual hierarchies) during a communion set at a table of wise teachers.

Upon receiving the offering of the aspirant, the wise spirit beings then offer spiritual food and drink to the aspirant to nourish their Higher-Self. This communion is replicated in the Holy Eucharist of Catholics and the Holy Communion of Christians. We feed the gods, and the gods feed us. But first, we must be prepared to be called to the 'wedding feast' of the spiritual hierarchies by cleansing our souls of the ugly karma that the Guardian's three beasts have shown us.

It is foolish to fight the Guardian of the Threshold because eventually every soul will resolve their unconscious actions, feelings, and thoughts before they can consciously enter the spiritual world either by meditation, sleep, or death. Karma will be redeemed and 'paid in full' before the aspirant truly becomes an initiate; for initiation is a way to consciously resolve karma before crossing the threshold of death. In light of this, most initiation rituals involve some form of mock death and resurrection back to life. In other words, a deep ritual enactment to serve as a meditation that resembles the steps the soul and spirit take after death. Through initiation, the aspirant replicates the hero's descent into the terrifying underworld and the attempt to return to the land of the living without having eaten or drank anything from the 'land of the shades.' Often, like the Sumerian goddess Inanna's descent into the underworld, we must discard anything from the physical world that holds us back: our crown, our scepter, our sword, our cloak, our shoes, our jewelry, and all of the other 'baggage' we may have brought with us from the land of the living.

We must go naked and completely transparent before the Guardian and beg his help to lighten our physical load before crossing into the spirit world that is the antithesis of material world—the illusion of Maya. This can be done in steps taken each night before we go to sleep by reviewing our daily thoughts, feelings, and deeds in a backward panorama. The key is to relive the day from the perspective of selflessness, from what effect your actions had upon the people you encountered. For once we see the effects we had on others, we begin to sense the karma (whether good or bad) that arises from each thought, feeling, or deed. This is a simple way to prepare to meet the Guardian with a little less fear of the evil our unconscious deeds have created. Once we review the day, we then can plan to rectify any lack of compassion we dealt out during the day, and thus lighten the load we bring before the Guardian.

One might assume that these somewhat scary and painful realities of the threshold might depict the Guardian as our personal enemy and a being who is negative. Actually, it is the exact opposite. The Guardian was created because humans work simultaneously with the spiritual hierarchy in our thinking, feeling, and willing creating elemental beings (in the three Elemental Kingdoms); thereby weaving together a memory body that aggregates all of our earthly deeds. These sense perceptible realities build up our karmic body with the impressions of the dense, gross material substance that is not allowed to pass the threshold and enter the spiritual world. For only spiritual substance is allowed into the spirit world, and we gain that spiritual soul substance through our higher thinking (Moral Imagination), higher feeling (Moral Inspiration), and higher deeds (Moral Intuition).

Imagination, Inspiration, and Intuition are spiritual substances loaned to humans in the physical world to help them ascend back to the place humans were created—the spiritual world.

In the Catholic Church, they have a sacrament of Confession which is much like a gentle meeting of the Guardian. A Roman Catholic examines his conscience and finds any sins he needs to 'get off this chest', and then he confesses those transgressions to the priest in the confessional booth. The priest then gives penance—actions that need to take place before the sin is truly released from the heart of the sinner. Often this involves saying prayers, making amends, or any other penance the priest finds fitting to help resolve the misdeed. This is a great thing to do regularly throughout life, whether you go to a priest or not.

Objective confession of your shortcomings and bad deeds, with a contrite heart, takes the stress and burden from the person confessing. Especially if you try to see the effects of your deeds upon others. We must learn to experience our self from the perspective of the other person. This is an enlightening exercise that should be done every night before you go to sleep. It is similar to the person who kneels beside their bed every night and prays before going to sleep. Eventually, after doing this type of soul searching every night for years, you learn to do it throughout the day. The gift of understanding the karmic consequences of your thoughts, feelings, and deeds can then blossom in the soul and the usual selfishness can be refined into selflessness and the results of your actions can be understood in the moment.

Jesus of Nazareth told us that, "It is easier for a camel to go through the eye of a needle than for a rich man to enter the kingdom of God." *Matthew* (19:24) The weight of materialism drowns the soul in physical considerations and blinds the spirit. The shadow-thinking of brain-bound materialists are actually pseudo thoughts not worthy of being offered to the spirit. Material considerations of self-aggrandizement often lead to the path of perdition and the Seven Deadly Sins. After that, the materialist sees no God in the Universe, no life after death, no life before birth, and a torturous physical world that is cold, heartless, and meaningless. Indeed, this type of materialism causes a person to faint when he comes anywhere near the Guardian.

Often materialists have no dreams and thus no 'food of the gods' to revive their spirit through sleep. They fear death, and worship only idols. After death, they will not ascend (expand) into the harmonious spheres surrounding the Earth and make their eternal offerings to the spiritual hierarchies. They will simply get what their materialistic shadow-thoughts have convinced them they will get—nothingness. If you can't feed the gods, they cannot feed you in return. Thus, materialists are in a living hell that is self-created and self-perpetuated. When they die and meet the Guardian of the Threshold and the Lord of Karma, they might actually believe they have 'gone to hell.'

There is no time to waste in cleaning out the 'garbage' accumulated in your double, in all three parts—physical, etheric, and astral. Ideally a deep meditation that creates transcendence beyond the threshold should be performed as a daily discipline, on a very regular schedule. Before sleep and upon awakening are the best times for meditation, contemplation, prayer, and spiritual communion. Even using the time just before confronting the Guardian, when imaginative mental pictures flow freely, can help purify the body of desires we carry as Earthly gravity that 'clip' the wings of spirit.

Meditation and death are two ways to meet the Guardian; but there are other occasions also. Often, a drowning person will see his 'life flash before him' in great detail—seeing the entire life in amazing images that seem to have been lost to the conscious mind. This happens because the etheric body (life body) is filled with memories that rise-up when the etheric body separates from the physical body through an accident, shock, or even consciously through spiritual initiation. The etheric body does the same thing when we die; it plays the record of everything we have ever done in a backwards order from the present to the past. This also happens in a small way each night as the day's memories replay themselves from the present backwards. This is what is called in science, the Rapid Eye Movement (REM) segment of sleep that happens every night. We have no choice in the matter of replaying our day, or our life, once we approach the Guardian, it is simply the way the etheric body processes memories.

Initiation entails loosening the etheric body from the physical so that thoughts can rise into the realm of active, living Imagination; within the realm of the Angels. In the past, this was done with metallic potions, shocking initiations of ritual death, long years of training, renunciation, or initiation in a one of another of the mystery schools that are found ubiquitously in every culture. The main question these initiations answered was: *What happens after death?* This question is answered in a small way each night when we sleep, or every time we can consciously cross the threshold (once we are purified of our earthly 'baggage') through transcendent meditation, prayer, or union with the divine. Unfortunately, the methodologies of initiation from the past do not work well in the present.

The point of initiation is the 'death of the lesser-self'; accomplished through a ritual 'death' of our personal selfishness that has led us to wrongdoing, evil, and death of the soul and spirit. For attachment to the physical world, self-pleasure, and the lower desires all add to the karmic debt that must be paid. Diminishing the load of materialistic shadow-thoughts, selfish emotional desire, and wrongful deeds that enslave human willpower causes the Guardian to grow smaller and smaller, and thus creates a smoother transition over the threshold. Consciously working on freeing the soul from earthly karmic 'gravity' is part of the path to initiation. It does not require a priest, guru, or wise-one to lead you on this path. For the fearful Guardian and his revelations are as close as your own heart. You don't have to go to a church, temple, or holy place physically to find your heart or your conscience. *You are the holy temple, the inner sanctum, the Threshold to the Spiritual World.* You can become the master of your own karma and right the wrongs you do every day by reflecting on your thinking, feeling, and willing and aligning them with the divine, to the eternal virtues found in love through truth, beauty, and goodness.

This book provides an opportunity to refine the reader's Language of the Spirit as it applies to initiation and the meeting of the Guardian of the Threshold that is so crucial in spiritual advancement. Of course, Dr. Rudolf Steiner, the brilliant clairvoyant seer, has given us the clearest expressions concerning the nature of the Guardian. This is because he experienced both the Lesser and Greater Guardians of the Threshold directly through his clairvoyance. Others, like H. P. Blavatsky, Alice A. Bailey, Dr. Franz Hartmann, and Sir Edward Bulwer-Lytton all spoke of the Guardian out of their philosophies, with some clairvoyant insight. Nonetheless, the confusion about the Guardian of the Threshold as taught by these teachers cannot be compared to what Steiner shared out of his spiritual scientific, clairvoyant perception of the Guardian. Notwithstanding, these authors offer different views (Languages of the Spirit) that can help the aspirant form an understanding of what one must, by necessity, encounter on the path to the spiritual world. For the limited views of theosophical speculation can lead one to the threshold, even though it may not necessarily lead one across into the spiritual world.

Every person who speaks out of direct knowledge of Spirit-Land will accurately describe the Guardian and place that being in a cosmology of hierarchical, divine spiritual beings. Ultimately, the Guardian is a map to the path of spiritual development, and later is found to be our own personal creation that must be worked with before we can clearly commune with our Guardian Angel. The Guardian of the Threshold can become the midwife for our 'spirit-birth' into the angelic world. Then, we find that this fearful, terrifying Guardian can lead us to our beautiful Guardian Angel, once we are pure enough to behold the spiritual world.

When we meet the Guardian at first, thinking, feeling, and willing separate and are torn asunder like the image of the three-headed dog Cerberus in ancient Greek mystery wisdom. Aspirants feel as if their own identity (ego) will be ripped apart permanently if they cannot find a way to hold the three parts of their soul together as they cross the threshold. Generally, in life, people do not even know they have three soul capacities that often go in different directions. One may have a good thought, but feelings might go in another direction, and then ultimately the person does something (willing) different than what they thought or felt. Confusion, stress, illness, and disinterest in the spirit are often the result of this chaotic soul condition. This condition is, in fact, an outcome of our time.

Humanity, as a whole, has been drawn across the threshold as the wisdom of the spirit is shared with humanity in divine inspirations flowing from the spiritual world to the faithful who are awake to the spirit. We now have access to parts of the spirit world that were sealed from humanity's perception in the past. Unfortunately, humanity has desecrated much of that spiritual wisdom and chosen, in many cases, materialism and anti-spiritual paths that cannot pass through this threshold. We should not forget that both good and bad may approach the doorway of the threshold. This dilemma of our times demonstrates the need for the Archangel Michael (now Archai Michael) to join our efforts in taming the dragon (Guardian) of our lower desires. This is the 'War in Heaven' that has now fallen to the Earth.

The battle for the soul and spirit of humanity rages while materialists have no idea that the future is being fought over in the realms of personal thinking, feeling, and willing. Each soul is now challenged to find their spirit and develop new supersensible organs of perception that enable the initiate to merge the three divergent soul elements into one cohesive whole, directed by a spiritual Higher-Self. This underscores the necessity of the individual to start their own self-initiation process immediately so that they will not be overwhelmed by the collective crossing of the threshold that humanity is going through on a global scale.

Every day, humanity is seeing new aberrations of thinking, feeling, and willing that have never been imagined before. The assault of the 'dragon of materialism' seems to be winning the War in Heaven that has fallen to Earth. The most grotesque displays of anti-human behavior seem to be pulling humanity back into the realms of animality instead of into the higher realms of the angelic hosts. It is world karma that we must now face through the unconscious evil that humanity has created.

This is the 'Global Guardian' who holds the karmic indebtedness of all the wars, hatred, and cruelty that humans have done to other humans and the world. Only through the Lord of Karma can the evil of the Global Guardian be dealt with; but the individual initiate can mitigate their personal karma and then work on the karma of their nation and then global humanity.

One of the most common references to the Guardian of the Threshold names the being the 'Dweller of the Threshold.' The Dweller of the Threshold was the literary invention of the English mystic and novelist Edward Bulwer-Lytton found in his novel *Zanoni* (1842). After the founding of the Theosophical Society in 1875, the term was widely used in theosophical circles as many teachers attempted to describe the nature of this being. According to Theosophy, the Guardian of the Threshold is a spectral figure that is the keeper of the karmic debit and credit 'ledger' of the individual. The Guardian is a menacing figure that is described by many esoteric teachers as manifesting itself as soon as the student of the spirit ascends upon the path into the higher worlds of spirit.

Rudolf Steiner speaks about this being called the Guardian of the Threshold in *An Outline of Occult Science, Knowledge of the Higher Worlds, The Secrets of the Threshold, The Mystery Dramas,* and *The First Class of Spiritual Science,* among other lectures and writings. According to Steiner's teachings, this Guardian will present itself as soon as the student of the spirit seeks the higher worlds. At a certain stage of evolution, the soul forces of thinking, feeling, and willing dissociate themselves and bring to the student a new inner way of perceiving that will lead to the encounter of the Guardian of the Threshold, who is also called the Doppelgänger or Double.

The Guardian of the Threshold stands before the supersensible world in order to deny entrance to those who are not truly ready to enter. The Guardian of the Threshold may be encountered in deep meditation and also when we pass through physical death. Rudolf Steiner identified both the Lesser and Greater Guardians and taught that, as a further development arising since the Mystery of Golgotha, Christ has now become within our Epoch the *Greater Guardian of the Threshold*, or '*the new Lord of Karma*.'

> "It consists in the fact that a certain office in the Cosmos, connected with the evolution of humanity in the twentieth century, passes over in a heightened form to the Christ. Occult clairvoyant research tells us that in our epoch Christ becomes the Lord of Karma for human evolution."
>
> Rudolf Steiner, From *Jesus to Christ*, Lecture III,
> *Sources of Knowledge of Christ, Lord of Karma*,
> Karlsruhe, October 7, 1911, GA 131

Furthermore, Rudolf Steiner tells us that the student meets the *Lesser Guardian of the Threshold* when the threads connecting willing, feeling, and thinking within the finer astral (desire) and etheric (life) bodies begin to loosen and go in different directions at the threshold to the spiritual world. While the Greater Guardian is encountered when this sundering of the connections extends to the physical parts of the body at death.

The founder of the Theosophical Society, Helena Petrovna Blavatsky, tells us that:

"Dwellers (on the Threshold). A term invented by Bulwer
Lytton in *Zanoni*; but in Occultism the word 'Dweller' is an
occult term used by students for long ages past, and refers to
certain maleficent astral Doubles of defunct persons."

H. P. Blavatsky *Theosophical Glossary* (1892)

In this view, the Dweller is also the shell of the previous
incarnation of a materialistic person discarded by the Higher Ego,
which is attracted to it in its new incarnation. (Theosophy.wiki)

"In rarer cases, however, something far more dreadful may
happen. When the lower Manas is doomed to exhaust
itself by starvation; when there is no longer hope that
even a remnant of a lower-light will, owing to favorable
conditions—say, even a short period of spiritual aspiration
and repentance—attract back to itself its Parent Ego, then
Karma leads the Higher Ego back to new incarnations. In
this case, the Kama-Manasic spook may become that which
we call in Occultism the 'Dweller on the Threshold.' This
'Dweller' is not like that which is described so graphically
in *Zanoni*, but an actual fact in nature and not a fiction
in romance, however beautiful the latter may be. Bulwer
must have got the idea from some Eastern initiate. Our
'Dweller,' led by affinity and attraction, forces itself into the
astral current, and through the Auric Envelope of the new
tabernacle inhabited by the Parent Ego, and declares war
to the lower-light which has replaced it. This, of course,
can only happen in the case of the moral weakness of the
personality so obsessed. No one strong in his virtue, and
righteous in his walk of life, can risk or dread any such thing;
but only those depraved in heart."

H. P. Blavatsky, *Collected Writings, Vol. XII. (1982; Pg. 636)*

Blavatsky's Eastern Theosophical terminology put most people off; but what she has indicated in the selections above shows that she herself did not directly experience the Dweller (Guardian) and can only speak philosophically about this being that is so personal and close to the aspirant. Blavatsky also points out that Bulwer-Lytton was simply writing about something someone had told him. Sir Edward Bulwer-Lytton wrote many novels, some of which have spiritual themes that reflect the occultism of his day. Nevertheless, he does not appear to have been a true initiate, even though he was 'initiated' in numerous secret societies. Consequently his view of the 'Dweller' is distorted and meant to scare more than instruct. This modern reference to the Dweller encouraged many theosophical teachers to write about the nature of this being.

Below is a selection of Bulwer-Lytton's *Zanoni* to give a flavor of what a novelist imagined the Dweller of the Threshold to look like. It is incorrect, as Blavatsky points out, and is the imagination of a 'novelist writing fiction.' While the fear and terror that can result from improperly meeting the Dweller is well communicated by Bulwer-Lytton; nonetheless, the true nature of the 'beast' eludes the author.

From: Sir Edward Bulwer Lytton, *Zanoni, A Rosicrucian Tale*, Book IV & V

"At last, Mejnour professed himself satisfied with the progress made by his pupil. 'The hour now arrives,' he said, 'when thou mayest pass the great but airy barrier—when thou mayest gradually confront the terrible Dweller on the Threshold. Continue thy labors—continue to suppress thine impatience for results until thou canst fathom the causes. I leave thee for one month; if at the end of that period, when I return, the tasks set thee are completed, and thy mind prepared by contemplation and austere thought for the ordeal, I promise thee the ordeal shall commence.'

"He could penetrate no further into the instructions; the cipher again changed. He now looked steadily and earnestly round the chamber. The moonlight came quietly through the lattice as his hand opened it, and seemed, as it rested on the floor and filled the walls, like the presence of some ghostly and mournful Power. He ranged the mystic lamps (nine in number), round the center of the room, and lighted them one by one. A flame of silvery and azure tints sprung up from each, and lighted the apartment with a calm and yet most dazzling splendor; but presently this light grew more soft and dim, as a thin gray cloud, like a mist, gradually spread over the room; and an icy thrill shot through the heart of the Englishman, and quickly gathered over him like the coldness of death. Instinctively aware of his danger, he tottered, though with difficulty, for his limbs seemed rigid and stone-like, to the shelf that contained the crystal vials; hastily he inhaled the spirit and laved his temples with the sparkling liquid. The same sensation of vigor, and youth, and joy, and airy lightness, that he had felt in the morning, instantaneously replaced the deadly numbness that just before had invaded the citadel of life. He stood with his arms folded on his bosom, erect and dauntless, to watch what should ensue.

"The vapor had now assumed almost the thickness and seeming consistency of a snow-cloud; the lamps piercing it like stars. And now he distinctly saw shapes, somewhat resembling in outline those of the human form, gliding slowly and with regular evolutions through the cloud. They appeared bloodless; their bodies were transparent and contracted or expanded, like the folds of a serpent. As they moved in majestic order, he heard a low sound—the ghost as it were of voice—which each caught and echoed from the other; a low sound, but musical, which seemed the chant of some unspeakable tranquil joy. None of these apparitions heeded him. His intense longing to accost them, to be of them, to make one of this movement of aerial happiness—for such it seemed to him—made him stretch forth his arms and seek to cry aloud, but only an inarticulate whisper passed his lips; and the movement and the music went on the same if the mortal were not there.

"Slowly they glided round and aloft, till, in the same majestic order, one after one, they floated through the casement and were lost in the moonlight; then, as his eyes followed them, the casement became darkened with some object undistinguishable at the first gaze, but which sufficed mysteriously to change into ineffable horror the delight he had before experienced. By degrees, this object shaped itself to his sight. It was as that of a human head, covered with a dark veil, through which glared with livid and demoniac fire, eyes that froze the marrow of his bones. Nothing else of the face was distinguishable—nothing but those intolerable eyes; but his terror, that even at the first seemed beyond nature to endure, was increased a thousand-fold, when, after a pause, the Phantom glided slowly into the chamber.

"The cloud retreated from it as it advanced; the bright lamps grew wane and flickered restlessly at the breath of its presence. Its form was veiled as the face, but the outline was that of a female; yet it moved not as move even the ghosts that simulate the living. It seemed rather to crawl as some vast misshapen reptile; and pausing, at length it cowered beside the table which held the mystic volume, and again fixed its eyes through the filmy veil on the rash invoker. All fancies, the most grotesque, of Monk or Painter in the early North, would have failed to give to the visage of imp or fiend that aspect of deadly malignity which spoke to the shuddering nature in those eyes alone.

Lucifer that arise in the etheric and astral bodies of the aspirant upon contacting the Guardian of the Threshold.

Lucifer appears in the astral body as a fallen Angel and Ahriman appears in the etheric body as a fallen Archangel. The Dweller is a combination of both of these and the 'Dragon' himself who is the combined effects of the fallen nature in the physical, etheric, and astral bodies. The Archai Michael keeps the Dragon at bay and eventually tames him, just as the Holy Spirit redeems Lucifer and the Father God will eventually redeem Ahriman. A third set of beings, the Asuras, are evil agents of the Sun-Demon Sorat's attempt to steal the ego ("I Am") of the individual. The Sun Being Christ redeems Sorat and the Asuras. Thus, the triple nature of the Guardian appears as three fallen beings, Lucifer-Ahriman-Asuras (Sorat) in the realms of thinking (astral), feeling (etheric), and willing (physical).

This elucidation of Rudolf Steiner makes clear the confusion Bailey had concerning the Dweller and the Angel of the Presence. Bailey obviously was channeling someone who was not experienced with the Guardian of the Threshold (Dweller) as it manifests in our modern times. Bailey does, however, give imaginative pictures of what is called the Double or Doppelgänger, which are other names and descriptions for the Guardian. It is instructive to study the differences between Bailey and Steiner. Steiner's ideas will be presented in the next section after Bailey's imaginative and romantic ideas about the Dweller.

Selections from Alice A. Bailey, *Glamour: A World Problem*

"The Dweller on the Threshold is usually regarded as presenting the final test of man's courage, and as being in the nature of a gigantic thoughtform or factor which has to be dissipated, prior to taking initiation. Just what this thoughtform is, few people know, but their definition includes the idea of a huge elemental form which bars the way to the sacred portal, or the idea of a fabricated form, constructed sometimes by the disciple's Master to test his sincerity. Some regard it as the sum total of a man's faults, his evil nature, which hinders his being recognized as fit to tread the Path of Holiness. None of these definitions, however, give a true idea of the reality.

"The Dweller on the Threshold is illusion-glamour-maya, as realized by the physical brain and recognized as that which must be overcome. It is the bewildering thoughtform with which the disciple is confronted when he seeks to pierce through the accumulated glamour of the ages and find his true home in the place of light.

"The Dweller on the Threshold, always present, swings however into activity only on the Path of Discipleship, when the aspirant becomes occultly aware of himself, of the conditions induced within him as a result of his interior illusion, his astral glamour and the maya surrounding his entire life. Being now an integrated personality, these three conditions are seen as a whole, and to this whole the term the 'Dweller on the Threshold' is applied. It is in reality a vitalized thoughtform—embodying mental force, astral force, and vital energy.

"The Dweller on the Threshold does not emerge out of the fog of illusion and of glamour until the disciple is nearing the Gates of Life. Only when he can catch dim glimpses of the Portal of Initiation and an occasional flash of light from the Angel of the Presence who stands waiting beside that door, can he come to grips with the principle of duality, which is embodied for him in the Dweller and the Angel. The day will come when you will stand, in full awareness, between these symbols of the pairs of opposites, with the Angel on the right and the Dweller on the left. May strength then be given to you to drive straight forward between these two opponents, who have for long ages waged warfare in the field of your life, and so may you enter into that

Rudolf Steiner's Indications on the Guardian of the Threshold

We often save the best for last, and in this instance, Rudolf Steiner's teachings on the Guardian of the Threshold are the best and go far beyond ancient philosophical and spiritual descriptions. Steiner gives details that help the aspirant understand the nature and being of the Guardian in modern times. We have arranged the selections of Rudolf Steiner below in a specific order that can take someone unfamiliar with this topic through a step-by-step presentation of a comprehensive picture of one of the most important elements in spiritual development. All paths of initiation go through the Guardian of the Threshold. Every human being must pass through the Guardian at death and each night upon falling asleep.

The Guardian is much bigger than a story in a novel or the theosophical work of Blavatsky, Bailey, or ancient spiritual texts because the Dweller must be described in a modern Language of the Spirit that updates prior descriptions and includes all that has been added to the collective 'Global Guardian of the Threshold' from modern humanity. Only Rudolf Steiner has given a complete cosmological understanding of the entire nature of the Guardian in the past, present, and future. Those seeking self-initiation through a new form of mystery wisdom can find it by studying and applying the knowledge Steiner gave in his Anthroposophy. Through working with these spiritual insights, the aspirant will find a solid path that goes directly to the summit.

As in the volumes in this series, the best way to understand anthroposophy is to let Rudolf Steiner explain topics in his own words. To gain a comprehensive perspective on the subject of the larger context of the Dweller on the Threshold within Spiritual Science we begin this section by including a complete lecture; therefore, as in other volumes in this series, it won't be surrounded by quotation marks; but rather, it will be preceded and followed by a triangle.

$$\Delta$$

Old and New Methods of Initiation, **Rudolf Steiner,
Lecture IV,** *Intimate aspects of soul and spiritual life—
Crossing the threshold—Contrast between West and East,*
Mannheim, January 19, 1922, GA 210

Some time has passed since we met here, and the opportunity to discuss a number of things with you after such a long while gives me the profoundest pleasure. Behind, us lie extremely grave times, difficult times, of which the gravity is certainly felt, though in wider circles it is still insufficiently understood. It is true to say that people who have experienced the second decade of the twentieth century have gone through more than is otherwise experienced over a span of centuries. We are asleep in our souls if we fail to notice how everything to do with human evolution is different now than it was ten years ago. The whole great turnabout that has taken place will no doubt only be fully realized by mankind at large after some time has passed. Then we shall come to see how the events that took place so catastrophically at the surface of life reach deep down into the roots of human souls, and how what has happened came about in the first instance as body. But, in death, *the wishes have also died.* Human beings enter the world-thoughts. As beings of spirit and soul they now have a thought life; but if they were to enter death entirely unprepared they would enter the same world as the one we enter when we go to sleep in the evening. To express this in extreme terms we have to say: If human beings enter death unprepared they find themselves in a terrible situation; for they have to watch what happens to their physical body. Their physical body is pulverized in the *World-All*; for if we do not cremate the body then it is cremated by the Cosmos. And human beings would have to watch this happening if they were unprepared.

What is the consequence of this, and what has to happen so that human beings see not only destruction after death, so that they live not only in the midst of destructive forces? By absorbing spiritual content, by developing a worldview which is consistent with the spirit, they must carry an inward relationship with the divine, spiritual world through the portal of death. If they are aware solely of a physical, material world, *then they certainly enter after death in a state of terrible unpreparedness into the world of destructive forces as though into a world of scorching flames.* But if they fill themselves with ideas and thoughts about the spiritual world, then the flames become the birthplace of the spirit after death so that they see not destruction alone; in the falling away of earthly dust from their human orbit they see the spirit rising up. No one should say what ordinary materialistic ideas are so prone to saying: *I can wait until death comes to me!* No, we must bear our consciousness of the spiritual world with us through the portal of death. Then with our soul and spirit we can overcome the destructive cosmic forces which take over our body, so that our element of spirit and soul rises up with new creativity above the destruction.

I am telling you this on the basis of anthroposophical
Spiritual Science, but you have all, surely, heard of the fear
experienced in former times in a sense of doom with regard to
death, a sense of doom about which the Apostle Paul[2] taught
when he spoke about man's soul being saved from falling a prey
to death. In former times people knew that they could not only
die physically with their corpse; but also spiritually with their
soul. Human beings dislike speaking about the possible death
of their soul. When speaking of death Paul does not mean
physical death. He means something that can happen because
physical death wants to lead on to the death of soul and spirit.
Human beings must become aware once more that they have to
do something during their physical earthly life in order to join
their consciousness to their soul and spirit, so that these may
carry something through death, in order that the spirit may
arise for them out of the devouring flames which are always
present after death.

Considerations like this must make it clear that to live within
the whole universal order is an immensely serious matter. No
view of the world is worthy of the human being if it does not
lead through inner strength to a world of moral values, if it does
not put before our souls the utter seriousness of life. To speak
of physical and chemical forces building up the Earth and of
living creatures and, finally, man developing along the way, is not
merely a one-sided worldview; it is a worldview which ignores the
seriousness of life and which arises, actually, simply out of human
laziness. A worldview, on the other hand, which achieves a proper
attitude to the spirit, leads to a seriousness about life because
it puts before the soul the possibility that on passing through
the gate of death the human being might become united with
the forces of destruction. Throughout their physical life human

But its inner forces are not then strong enough to bring about consciousness of itself.

"In order to understand clairvoyant experience, especially in its early beginnings, it is particularly important to bear in mind that the soul may already have begun to live in the supersensible world before it is able to formulate to itself any knowledge worthy of the name. Clairvoyance at first appears in a very subtle way, so that often, inasmuch, as they expect to see something almost tangible, people do not heed clairvoyant impressions which are flitting-by, and will in no way recognize them as such. In this case the impressions sink into oblivion almost as soon as they appear. They enter the field of consciousness so slightly that they remain quite unnoticed, like tiny clouds on the soul's horizon.

"On this account, and because people for the most part expect clairvoyance to be quite different from what it at first is, it often remains undiscovered by many earnest seekers after the spiritual world. In this respect too he meeting with the Guardian of the Threshold is important. If the soul has been strengthened just in the direction of self-knowledge, this very meeting may merely be like the first gentle flitting-by of a spiritual vision; but it will not be so easily consigned to oblivion as other supersensible impressions, because people are more interested in their own being than in other things.

"There is, however, no need at all that the meeting with the Guardian should be one of the first clairvoyant experiences. The soul may be strengthened in various directions, and the first of such directions may bring other beings or events within its spiritual horizon before the meeting with the Guardian takes place. Yet this meeting is sure to occur comparatively soon after entering the supersensible world."

Brunetto Latini, Rudolf Steiner, Dornach, January 30, 1915, GA 161

"Man, to begin with, on the Earth, is for himself the only example—the only document he has brought over from the spiritual world. Therefore he must pass through this, the document of his own being. He must go through himself. This was always known to those who experienced anything of Initiation. Thus it was known to Brunetto Latini, teacher and friend of Dante. Moreover, it is characteristic how Brunetto Latini's Initiation, as we may call it, was eventually brought about. It happened by a particular event. That is what frequently occurs. Fundamentally speaking, everyone who sets his foot on the path of Spiritual Science is waiting for the portal of the spiritual world to be opened to him sooner or later, as indeed it will be. It may be—indeed it often is so—that the entry to the spiritual world takes place by degrees. Then we grow slowly into the spiritual world. Nevertheless, very, very frequently it happens that the world is opened to us as by a kind of shock which breaks in upon our life—*by a sudden and unexpected event.*"

Errors in Spiritual Investigation: Meeting the Guardian of the Threshold, Rudolf Steiner, Berlin, March 6, 1913, GA 62

"From what has been said in preceding lectures, it should be clear that all spiritual training consists of an awakening of certain spiritual forces that exist in the soul but that slumber in ordinary life and must be developed. The spiritual organs and the supersensible consciousness can be developed only when forces lying peacefully in the depths of the soul, forces that are weak or not at all developed in ordinary life, are really brought into consciousness.

"The following can be seen from what has been said. Two things appear when man, through appropriate meditation, through concentrating his whole life of soul on individual mental images called into consciousness by his free will, tries to draw forth these forces resting in the depths of his soul. First, a quality that is always present in the soul but that in ordinary life can be kept relatively in check will be intensified, along with the other slumbering qualities in the depths of the soul; spiritual development cannot take place in any other way than by the whole soul life becoming in a certain respect inwardly more active, more infused with energy. This quality that is intensified at the same time as the others that one is trying directly to intensify one can call human self-love, sense-of-self. One could say that one begins to know this human self-love, this sense-of-self, only when one goes through a spiritual scientific training; only then does one begin to know how deep within the human soul this self-love slumbers. As has been pointed out already, he who engages in the exercises described in past lectures, thus intensifying his soul forces, notices at a certain moment in his development that another world enters his soul life. He must be able to notice, to have the knowledge to recognize, that the first form (Gestalt) in which the new, supersensible world appears is nothing other than a projection, a shadow image, of his own inner soul life. These forces that he has developed in his soul life appear to him first in a mirror image. This is the reason that the materialistic thinker easily mistakes what appears in the soul life of the spiritual investigator for what can appear in the unhealthy soul life as illusions, visions, hallucinations, and the like. That objections from this side rest on ignorance of the facts has often been pointed out; this distinction, however, must be alluded to again and again. The unhealthy soul life, which beholds its own essence as in a mirror image, takes its own reflections for a real world and is not in a position to eliminate these reflections through inner choice. By comparison, in a true spiritual training it must be maintained that the spiritual investigator recognizes the first phenomena that appear as reflections of his own being; not only does he recognize them as such, but he is able to eliminate them, to extinguish them from his field of consciousness.

"Just as the spiritual investigator is able through his exercises to intensify his soul forces so that a new world is conjured before him, so he must be able to extinguish this whole world in its first form; he must not only recognize it as a reflection of his own being but be able to extinguish it again. If he could not extinguish it, he would be in a situation comparable to something that occurs in sense observation and that would be unbearable, impossible in an actual development of the human soul. Imagine in ordinary sense observation that a person directed his eyes to an object and became so attracted to it that he could not avert his gaze. The person would not be able to look around freely but would be tied to the object. This would be an unbearable situation in relation to the outer world. With a spiritual development, it would mean exactly the same in relation to the supersensible world if a person were not in the position to turn from his spiritual observation and extinguish what presents itself as image to his spiritual observation. He must pass the test expressed in the words, 'You are able to extinguish your image,' overcoming himself in this extinguishing; if the image returns, so that he can know his reality in a corresponding way, then only does he face reality and not his own imaginings (Einbildung). The spiritual investigator therefore must be able not only to create his own spiritual phenomena and to approach them but also to extinguish them again.

is unaware of it in ordinary life only because he does not have the appropriate organs to perceive it. The spiritual world surrounds us always and is always behind that which the senses perceive. Before man can enter this world, however, he must strengthen his ego, his I. With the strengthening of the ego, however, the aforementioned qualities also appear. He therefore must learn above all else to know himself, so that when he is able to confront a spiritual outer world in the same way as he confronts an objective being he can distinguish for himself what is the truth. If he does not learn to delimit himself in this way, he will always confuse that which is only within him, that which is only his subjective experience, with the spiritual world picture; therefore, he can never arrive at a real grasp of spiritual reality.

"To what extent fear plays a certain role upon entering the spiritual world can be observed particularly in the people who deny the existence of such a world. We must now emphasize that the soul life of the human being is, as it were, twofold. In the soul not only does there exist what man ordinarily knows; but in the depths of the soul life things are happening that cast their shadows—or their lights—into ordinary consciousness. Ordinary consciousness, however, does not reach down to this level. We can find in the hidden depths of soul hatred and love, joy and fear and excitement, without our carrying these effects into conscious soul life. It is therefore entirely correct to say that a phenomenon of hatred directed from one person to another, taking place within consciousness, actually can be rooted, in the depths of soul, in love. There can be a sympathy, a deep sympathy, of one person for another in the depths of the soul, but since this person at the same time has reasons—reasons about which he perhaps knows nothing—he is confused about this love, about the sympathy, deceiving himself with hatred and antipathy. This is something that holds sway in the depths of the soul, so that these depths look quite different from what we call our everyday consciousness. There can be conditions of fear, of anxiety, in the depths of the soul of which one has no conscious idea. Man can have that fear in the depths of his soul, that anxiety in face of the spiritual world—because he must cross the abyss that has been described before entering—and yet be aware of nothing consciously. Actually, all human beings who have not yet entered the spiritual world—but who have acquired an understanding of entering, have to a degree this fear, this terror in face of the spiritual world. Whatever one may think concerning this fear and anxiety that are within the depths of the soul, they are there, though they appear stronger with one person, weaker with another. Because the soul might be injured, man is protected by the wisdom-filled nature of his being from being able to look further into the spiritual world, from being able to have the experience of meeting the Guardian of the Threshold until he is ready for it. Before that he is protected. Therefore, one speaks of the experience of the Guardian of the Threshold.

"We can note that a materialistically or monistically-minded person, although knowing nothing of this experience, does have this fear in face of the spiritual world in the depths of his soul. There lives in such a person a certain antipathy to confronting the abyss that must be crossed; and to help him get past this fear, this anxiety in the soul in face of the spiritual world, the monist or materialist thinks out his theories and denies the spiritual world; this denial is nothing other than a self-induced anesthesia in face of his fear. This is the real explanation for materialism. As unsympathetic as it may sound, for one who knows the soul it is evident that in a meeting of materialistic monists, or those who deny soul and spirit, there prevails only the fear in the face of the we arrive at a true conception of what a dream is. Thus we find how a dream is interpreted rightly only when we do not relate it to the physical, naturalistic world, but to the spiritual—above all, in most cases, to the moral world. The dream will never tell what it is expressing if its content is given a physical interpretation, but only when the interpretation is in accordance with the spiritually moral.

"To illustrate this, let us turn to the confusion of the dream I told you about yesterday—the dream in which someone going for a walk is suddenly overcome with shame at finding himself without clothes in a crowded street. I remarked how the whole mood of soul in dream-consciousness is due to our confronting three different worlds. Looking at a dream of this kind in the right way, however, we see that although its content appears to belong to the realm of the senses, yet through this medium the spiritual-moral is seeking to reveal itself. Hence, anyone having such a dream ought not to look at the immediate, symbolical course it takes, but should ask himself: Haven't I sometimes had a tendency in daytime consciousness not to be completely truthful about myself with others? Haven't I perhaps been too fond of following the fashion in what I wear—altogether too apt to take refuge in convention? Is it not a characteristic of mine to give people a false impression of what I really am?

"When anyone lets his thoughts take this course, he gradually arrives at the moral, spiritual interpretation of the dream. He says to himself: When during sleep I was in the supersensible world, I met with spiritual beings there—they told me that I should not be present in a cloak of falsehood—but *as I really am inwardly, in soul and spirit*.

"When we interpret dreams in this way, we come to their moral, spiritual truth. A whole host of dreams can be interpreted thus.

"People of an older chapter in history, who even in the dreamy symbolism of sleep were conscious of the Guardian of the Threshold, took to heart his warning not to carry with them what belongs to the physical world of the senses when they enter the spiritual world. Had these men dreamt they had no clothes on in the street, it would never have occurred to them that they ought to have been ashamed; this is something that holds good for the physical world, for a man's physical body. They would have given heed to the warning that what holds good for the physical does not hold good in the spiritual world, and that what appears in the spiritual world is being said to human beings by the Gods. A dream, therefore, had to be interpreted as an utterance of the Gods. Only during the course of human evolution have dreams come to be interpreted in a naturalistic sense...

"It will be clear from the descriptions I have been giving you that between the physical world of the senses and the spiritual, supersensible world, there is a barrier which with a certain rightness we call the *Threshold of the Spiritual World*.

"I have already pointed out in various ways how necessary it is that we should be able to cross this Threshold, and we have still to speak about it in greater detail. But you will have gathered already from my lectures that in older periods of human evolution this crossing of the Threshold was a rather different matter from what it is at the present day. In those ancient times people were able to cross in another way because even by day their consciousness was dreamlike, but for that very reason more alive to the supersensible. Thus, in the way I have pictured, they passed the Guardian of the Threshold half-consciously, dreamily, both on going to sleep and on waking.

"Here we can see a transition from men of an older type, with little freedom, to those who were becoming increasingly free. This former determinism was bound up with the fact that on going to sleep, and on awaking, men had some perception of the Guardian of the Threshold, who stood there giving warning. Now, in place of this unfree situation, we have the incapacity of present-day consciousness to see into the spiritual world, which signifies an increasing freedom: *herein lies a principle of human progress.*"

"Hence we can say that, looked at from the spiritual world, people have lost a great deal precisely because in the course of their evolution they have had to be led towards freedom. What has been lost, however, must be regained, in the way that Anthroposophy, for example, would show. And now is the historical point of time when a striving to regain what has been lost must begin.

"But everywhere, among people of very various kinds, there still rises up something inherited from an earlier age, when man's relation to the spiritual world was different. So that today, in the consciousness of those given up to intellectualism, there is a strict frontier set up, as a rule, between what they experience in the world of the senses and what lies beyond in the spiritual world. The frontier is in fact so rigorously maintained that even enlightened spirits are unwilling to admit the possibility of crossing it.

"In my brief sketch of the way into the supersensible world, I have indicated that it is possible to cross the frontier and to enter that world in full consciousness. But as a relic from the time when a man entered the spiritual world in a more instinctive, unconscious way, and even in his day-consciousness had more in him of the spiritual world, there still rises up into his evolution today a certain heritage from the past. And this is something we must imperatively understand through conscious spiritual cognition. For, if not rightly understood, it manifests itself in many deceptive ways, and in these matters such errors can become very dangerous. Hence in the course of these lectures, intended to describe the evolution of man and of the world, I must speak about this question of a boundary, where what was natural and taken for granted among the people of former epochs re-appears today, and can lead to dangerous illusions in those who have not the requisite clear knowledge for dealing with it.

"Among these phenomena, situated for ordinary consciousness at the frontier between the sense-world and the supersensible, are *visions*. I mean the visions where, in a state of hallucination more or less controlled by the person concerned, pictures arise which have quite definite forms and colors—they may even seem to speak—but correspond to nothing external. For normal perception, the object is outside; the image, in a shadowy way within; and a person is perfectly conscious of how the shadowy, conceptual image is related to the external world. The vision arises of itself, claiming to be a reality on its own account. A person subject to such visions becomes incapable of estimating rightly what reality there is in the pictures which appear before him without his initiative.

"How, then do visions come about? They come about because the human being still possesses the capacity for carrying over into his waking world what he experiences during sleep, and of bringing it into conceptual form just as he does with his sense-perceptions. Whether, after perceiving a clock that exists physically for the senses, I make an inner picture of it, or whether, after experiencing in a dream the form and inner reality of an external object, I wake up and make a picture of my experience, the only difference between the two processes is that I am in control of one of them—hence the image of it is more shadowy and flat—while the other process is outside my control. In the latter case I carry nothing of the real present into my conceptual life; but something experienced when the soul was outside in a past—perhaps long past—sleep, *and out of this dream-experience I build up a vision.*

"In an earlier age of human evolution, when the relation of people both to the physical world and to the spiritual world was ruled by instinct, such visions were perfectly natural; it is human progress that has made them the uncontrolled, illusory things they are today. We must therefore be quite clear that modern man lacks something: when he has some experience in the spiritual world during sleep and is returning to the physical world, he no longer hears the warning of the Guardian of the Threshold:—

'All that you have experienced in the spiritual world you should note well and carry back to the physical world.'

"If he does carry it back, he will know what is contained in the vision. But if the vision appears to him only in the physical world, without his realizing that he has brought it back from the spiritual world, so that he fails to understand what it really is, then he is without guidance, and at the mercy of illusion where his visionary experience is concerned. So we can say: Visions come about because a man carries over unawares his sleep-experience into his waking life, and in his waking life he then forms conceptions of the experiences—conceptions which are much richer in content than the ordinary shadowy ones, and these he builds up into vivid visions complete with color and sound.

"Another thing that comes about is this. A man carries over into his life of sleep the feelings and perceptions of the kind he has in physical life. Then, when he is in the act of carrying this

over into the open sea of sleep-life, he is warned to be careful
not to do anything foolish. If the sleep is very light—a far more
common condition in ordinary life than is realized, for we are
often just a little asleep when walking about quite normally,
and we ought to be more aware of this—we may then, without
noticing it, carry over the Threshold our everyday faculty of
perception. Then arise those obscure feelings, as if one were
inwardly watching something happening in the future, either
to oneself or to someone else, and we have a *premonition*. Thus,
whereas a *vision* comes about when experience during sleep
is carried down into waking life and the threshold is crossed
unconsciously, *premonition* comes about when we are in a light
sleep without realizing it and, thinking we are awake, carry
over the Threshold, again ignoring the Guardian, our daytime
experience. This, however, lies so deep down in the subconscious
that it is not noticed. We are, of course, at all times connected
with the whole world; and if we could draw this knowledge up out
of the subconscious, we should be able to draw up much else also.

"You will now see how, because these legacies from the
evolutionary past can still be experienced, visions arise on one
side of the Threshold, premonitions on the other. But a man may
also halt at the Threshold and still not notice the Guardian. There
may then be moments when inwardly, in his soul, he is as if he
were enchanted. But the word 'enchanted' does not quite meet the
case, for he is not enchanted in the sense we generally associate
with the term—it is rather that his attitude of soul undergoes
a change. When he comes to the Threshold in such a way that
he still perceives what is in the physical world while already
perceiving what is in the supersensible, he experiences something
which is widespread in certain regions of the Earth—*second sight*,
a half-conscious experience at the Threshold. Hence to sum up

these legacies from the past, these phenomena in a man's life when his consciousness is dimmed, we have those appearing on this side of the Threshold as *visions*; those appearing beyond the Threshold as *premonitions*; those actually at the Threshold as *second sight.*"

Foundations of Esotericism, Rudolf Steiner, Lecture II, Berlin, September 27, 1905, GA 93a

"When a human being has progressed so far that he has transformed his entire etheric body, Devachan is no longer necessary. This is the case with the occult pupil who has perfected his development and who has transformed his etheric body so that it remains intact after death and has no need to pass through Devachan. This is called the renunciation of Devachan. It is permissible to allow someone to work on one's etheric body when one is certain that he no longer brings anything of evil into the rest of the world; otherwise he would work his harmful instincts into it. Under hypnosis it can happen that the one hypnotized works into the world the harmful instincts of the hypnotist. In the case of normal people the physical body prevents the etheric body from being dragged and drawn hither and thither. When however the physical body is in a state of lethargy it is possible for the etheric body to be worked into. If one person hypnotizes another and works harmful instincts into him, these also remain with him after death. Many of the practices of black magicians consisted in their creating willing servants by this means. It is the rule of white magicians to allow nobody to have his etheric body worked into unless by someone whose instincts have passed through catharsis. In the etheric body rest and wisdom prevail. When something bad enters into it, this element of evil comes to rest and therefore endures.

"Before the human being as pupil is led to that point at which of his own choice he can work on his etheric body, he must at least, to a certain extent be able to evaluate karma in order to achieve self-knowledge.

"Meditation therefore should not be undertaken without continual self-knowledge, self-observation. By this means, at the right moment man will behold the Guardian of the Threshold:— *the karma which he has still to pay back.* When one reaches this stage under normal conditions it merely signifies the recognition of his still existing karma.

"If I begin to work into my etheric body, I must make it my aim to balance my still remaining karma. It can happen that the Guardian of the Threshold appears in an abnormal way. This happens when a person is so strongly attracted to one particular life between birth and death, that because of the very slight degree of inner activity he cannot remain long enough in Devachan. If someone has accustomed himself to be too outward looking—*he has nothing to see within.* He then soon comes back into physical life. His desires remain present, the short Devachan is soon over, and when he returns, the collective form of his earlier desires still exists in Kamaloka; he comes up against this also. He incarnates. The old is then mingled with his new astral body. This is his previous karma, the Guardian of the Threshold. He then has his earlier karma continually before him. *This is a specific form of the Double.*

"Many of the popes of the notorious papal age, as for example Alexander VI, have had such a Double in their next incarnation. There are people, and at present this is not infrequent, who have their previous lower nature continually beside them. That is a special kind of insanity. It will become ever stronger and more threatening, because materialistic life becomes ever more widespread. Many people who now yield themselves up completely to materialistic life will in their next incarnation have the abnormal form of the Guardian of the Threshold at their side. If now the influence of spirituality were not to be very strongly exercised, a kind of epidemic would arise of seeing of the Guardian of the Threshold as the result of the materialistic civilization. Of this the neurotic tendency of our century is the precursor. It is a kind of losing oneself in the periphery. All the neurotics of today will be harassed by the Guardian of the Threshold in their next incarnation. They will be pursued by the difficulties resulting from a too early incarnation, a sort of cosmic premature birth. What we have to strive for in Theosophy is a sufficiently long time in Devachan—*in order to avoid incarnating too early.*

"From this aspect we must consider the entrance of Christ into world history. Previously, anyone who wished to achieve a life in Christ had to enter into a Mystery School. There a state of lethargy was induced in the physical body and only through the purified priesthood could there be added to the astral body what was still needed for its purification. This constituted initiation.

"But through the coming of Christ into the world, it came about that an individual who felt drawn to Christ could receive from Him something which could take the place of this old form of initiation. It is always possible that someone through union with Christ can preserve his astral body in so purified a condition that he is able to work into his etheric body without doing harm to the world. When one bears this in mind the expression 'vicarious atonement through death' receives quite a different new significance. For this is what is actually meant by the atoning death of Christ. As before this, death in the Mysteries had to be suffered by everyone who wished to obtain purification. Now the

One suffered for all, so that through the world-historic initiation a substitute has been created for the old form of initiation. Through Christianity much that is of a communal nature has been brought about; which previously was not communal. The active power of this substitution is expressed in the fact that through inner-vision, through true mysticism, community with Christ is possible.

"This has also been embodied in language. The first Christian initiate in Europe, Ulfilas,[1] himself embodied it in the German language, in that man found the 'Ich' within it. Other languages expressed this relationship through a special form of the verb, in Latin for instance the word 'amo'; but the German language adds to it the Ich. 'Ich' is J. Ch. = Jesus Christ. It was with intention that this was introduced into the German language. It is the initiates who have created language. Just as in Sanskrit the AUM expresses the Trinity, so we have the sign ICH to express the inmost-being of man. By this means a central-point was created whereby the tumultuous emotions of the world can be transformed into rhythm. Rhythm must be instilled into them through the Ich. This center-point is literally the Christ."

Note:

1. Ulfilas (c. 311-383) was a 4th century preacher of Cappadocian Greek descent. He was the apostle to the Gothic people; who oversaw the translation of the *Bible* into Gothic. Known as the *Gothic Bible* or *Wulfila Bible*, is the Christian *Bible* in the Gothic language spoken by the Eastern Germanic (Gothic) tribes in the Early Middle Ages. During the third century, the Goths lived on the Northeast border of the Roman Empire, in what is now Ukraine, Bulgaria and Romania. During the fourth century, the Goths were converted to Christianity, largely through the efforts of Bishop Wulfila, who is also believed to have invented the Gothic alphabet. The translation of the *Bible* into the Gothic language is thought to have been performed in Nicopolis ad

Istrum in today's Northern Bulgaria, and traditionally is attributed to
Wulfila.

Initiation, Eternity and the Passing Moment, Rudolf Steiner, Lecture IV, Munich, August 28, 1912, GA 138

"In literature you will find everywhere where mention is made
of initiation that the riddle of death, so closely concerning all
mankind, is, in some way or another, touched upon. In anything
of the nature of records you will find allusions to how at a certain
stage the initiate has to experience, in a somewhat different
form, how the passing is made through the gate of death. To
the occultist these records are actually founded on truth. The
experiences that have to be passed through during the ascent into
spiritual worlds are akin to the experiences man must undergo
in the natural crossing from life in the physical body to the
entirely different sheath found between death and a new birth.
If we would come to the essence of this matter in the right way,
we must first ask what man knows about himself in ordinary life.
Such an abstract question may not be of much interest; but for
an understanding of what takes place in initiates, it is necessary
to focus one's attention on the question, 'What does the soul
consider itself to be?'

"During sleep the soul does not know what it is because sleep
runs its course either in a state of unconsciousness, or dreams
play into it, which, to be rightly understood must be interpreted
by the occultist. So, in considering the questions, 'What is man?
What is his soul in ordinary sense existence?' we have to do
only with waking life. Now we know that in the first place there
are the gateways we call our sense organs, through which the
world of light and color, sound and smell, the world of heat and

cold, and so forth, stream into our souls. In the life of the senses what we call 'our world' is really only a gathering up of all that streams in through these sensory gateways. Then we have the instruments of our understanding, our feeling and willing, with which to work on what meets us in the outer world. Within our soul cravings and desires arise, strivings, states of satisfaction and dissatisfaction, joy, disillusion, and so on. Were we to envisage the whole compass of what man recognizes as himself, it is all this. If we want to know what the 'inner-world' is in ordinary life, we can in reality put forward nothing more than the whole of what has just been described. Moreover, man can also look at himself from outside. He can observe his own body. Through countless facts that need not here be dealt with in detail, he becomes aware that he must regard his body as the instrument for his waking life between birth and death. We have already touched upon the longings that play into this life. Among them is a longing to know what man really is within the limits of birth and death, the longing to issue forth from what may be called the darkness of life. But man has no direct experience in his ordinary life of the senses of how to do this. His experiences are such that the ebb and flow of impulses, cravings, sense impressions, ideas, intellectual connections, and so forth, completely fill his waking life. We can now link this to what was occupying us at the end of our last lecture.

"Attention was then drawn to the way in which man, on reaching the boundary between sense existence and spirit existence, has to alter his conceptions, how he must leave behind all his thoughts about the ugly and beautiful, true and false, good and bad, as these concepts take on quite another significance and a different kind of value within the spiritual worlds. From this we can get some idea of how we must change ourselves if we would

steps of initiation hangs on the memory in super-sensible life, on preserving the memory of ordinary life. Such a memory is indeed possible, and it is brought about through initiation. All this can be linked to the riddle of death.

"When a man passes through death, he has not the identical forces he acquired by initiation because, when he lays aside the body, he acquires certain forces through the help of beings of the super-sensible world. He gains the power to preserve in memory what in laying aside the body he has forgotten. Here you have the real answer to the question, 'What remains of the experiences of my soul when I have passed through the gate of death? How does my soul live on?' That is a question of the greatest importance, and through the experience of the initiates you have the answer, 'The soul lives on because in its hidden depths there are forces able to hold fast in memory what has been experienced.' To be immortal means having the power to preserve in memory the renounced past existence. That is the real definition of human immortality. Through initiation we have proof—experienced proof—that forces live in man that can remind him, after he has laid aside his physical body, of all that he has experienced in sensory life, and of anything at all that has happened. In this way the human self is preserved into the future; thus man experiences his former existence as memories in his future life. We should feel the whole power of the thought that is called forth by initiation, that could be expressed in the words, 'The human being is of such a nature that he bears his own being through future ages by the force of super-sensible memory.' If you feel this thought pouring with feeling into the void of the Universe, picturing the soul as it carries its own being through eternity, then you have a far better definition of what is called a monad than can be given through any philosophical concepts. Then you will feel what a monad is, that is, a self-enclosed being, a being carrying itself. It is only through the experiences of initiation that one can arrive at such conceptions.

"That is only one side of what I have been describing to you. We must consider its first steps more precisely if we want to approach with feeling what can give us ideas about initiation. Let us assume that a man has, through an attitude of soul strengthened by thought and meditation, come to the point of being able to perceive in his etheric body. This perception is experienced in the body that, in its several parts, is more closely bound up with the brain, and less closely, for example, with the hands. The feeling oneself into the etheric body is experienced in the sensation, 'You are being spread out. You are becoming wider, fleeing out into the boundless spaces of the Universe.' Such is the subjective feeling. This is not, however, that one rushes headlong into the unreal and the vague; everything there is concrete life. One lives oneself into the purely concrete, and in this widening out one comes at the same time to definite experiences. Except in special circumstances, hardly anyone accomplishing the first steps of initiation will be spared the experience of a particular impression or feeling of dread and anxiety, an experience of being in the vast Universe with no firm ground beneath one's feet, an oppression of the soul. This is the kind of inner experience one lives through.

"But there is something of still greater importance. In ordinary life we think, we have an idea, one thought suggests another, and we connect the one thought with the other, combining these perhaps with feelings, wishes, willing and so forth. In a sound life of the soul, one will always find it possible to say, 'I think this, I feel that.' Were we unable to speak thus, it would mean a break, a disturbance, in sound soul life. We

widen out, we expand when growing into the etheric body—
but at the same time our thoughts also expand. When thinking,
we lose the sensation of being within ourselves, and we get
the feeling that we are growing into the etheric world that is
permeated with thoughts that think themselves. That arises as
an actual experience. It is as if we ourselves were blotted out
and our thoughts were thinking themselves, as if the feelings we
ourselves have, or that things have, felt themselves, as if we could
not do our willing for ourselves but that all this was awakened
and willed in us. The feeling one has is one of being given up
to the objective, to the world. But, as a rule, another feeling is
added. This is another of the experiences during the first steps
of initiation. We have the feeling that, as we expand and widen
out, and our thoughts think themselves, feelings feel themselves,
in the same measure our consciousness becomes weaker and
weaker, more and more toned down, and our capacity for
knowing is deadened.

"Now for the soul to go through such experiences, one must
allow something quite definite to enter it. It is necessary for these
things to be grasped by the soul as accurately as possible. For this
reason I have collected a few things—if not the same, of a similar
nature and tending in the same direction—in the book *A Road
to Self Knowledge.* (GA 16) If you take it in connection with these
lectures, you may gain a good deal. A quite definite state of soul,
produced by oneself, must come about similar to what I described
yesterday. One must practice self-observation and try to bring
home to oneself, without either mercy or consideration, the really
grievous faults one knows oneself to possess, so that there comes
before the soul a feeling, into which one must live deeply, of how
little one corresponds to the great ideal of humanity. With real
force of thought and meditation, one's moral weakness, all one's

weaknesses, must be called up before the soul. So doing, one will become stronger. What has already begun to be deadened, what has been described as a kind of fading out of the soul, brightens up again. It once more begins to be visible.

"At this point something can be experienced that finds easy expression in words, but is oppressive and even disturbing during the first stages of initiation. These words all apply to the life of soul and not to life in the body. For anyone who has been led properly into the spiritual worlds, will already have received intimation that there is no question of external bodily danger. Such a man, if he faithfully observes the good advice offered him, can remain externally the same man in life, in spite of the ebb-and-flow within him of every sort of pain, torment and disillusion, among which may also be premonitions of bliss. Such things must be gone into because in them lie the seeds of a higher vision, of a higher insight. In this way one gradually comes to recognize that by learning to observe, to perceive and to experience independently of the physical body—in other words, learning to live in the etheric body—one grows into the etheric world in the way described. But in so doing one learns the reason why this etheric world fades into a kind of unconsciousness. In simple words we might say, 'It does not like me; it does not think me suited for it.' This deadening, this vanishing away, is merely the expression for, 'They will not let me in!' But in dwelling on one's faults one grows stronger, and what had begun to disappear lights up again. This produces, however, the significant feeling that a super-sensible world of an etheric nature is around one; but that it may only be entered to a certain degree. It will only allow one to enter to the degree that one makes oneself increasingly strong, morally and intellectually. Otherwise, no. And it shows you this by fading away before you.

guardian of the threshold, is one of the tasks of the moment and of the immediate future."

$$\Delta$$

Threshold in Nature and In Man, **Rudolf Steiner,** *The Human Soul and the World of Nature,* **Basle, February 1, 1921, GA 80b**

"In olden times, these two aims—knowledge of Nature and knowledge of self—were associated in the mind of man with quite strange, not to say terrifying, conceptions. It was indeed not thought possible for man to continue in his ordinary way of life if he wanted to set out on the path to knowledge; for on that path, he would inevitably find himself in the presence of deep uncertainties before he could come to any satisfying conviction...

"They beheld a kind of abyss between what man is and can experience in ordinary life, and what he becomes and is confronted with when he penetrates into the depths of world-existence, or into the knowledge of his own being. They described how man feels the ground sink away from under his feet, so that only if he be strong enough not to succumb to giddiness of soul can he go forward at all into the field of ultimate knowledge. To tread this path of knowledge unprepared would involve man in a harder test than he is able to meet. Serious and conscientious preparation was necessary before he dare bridge the abyss. In ordinary life man is unaware of the abyss—*he simply does not see it.* And that, they said, is for him a blessing. Man is enveloped in a kind of blindness that protects him from being overcome by giddiness and falling headlong into the abyss. They spoke too of how man had to cross a 'Threshold' in order to come into the fields of higher knowledge, and of how he must have become able to face without fear the revelations that await him at the Threshold. Again, in ordinary life man is protected from crossing the Threshold. Call it personification or what you will, in those ancient schools of wisdom they were relating real experiences when they spoke of man being protected by the 'Guardian of the Threshold,' and of undergoing beyond it a time of darkness and uncertainty before ultimately attaining to a vision of reality, a 'standing within' spirit-filled reality...

"It is important to grasp the significance of this fact. What is common knowledge today, freely spoken of by everyone, was in earlier times a wisdom known to a select few. What the wisdom-pupil knew, for example, concerning the Sun and its relation to the Earth was considered a knowledge that lay 'beyond the Threshold'; man must needs first cross the Threshold before he can come into those fields where the soul discovers this new relationship to the Universe. The very same knowledge that our whole education renders familiar and natural to us today, was for them on the other side of a Threshold that must not be crossed without due preparation.

"This accounts for the emphasis on the training of the will; for a strong and vigorous will strengthens also the consciousness of self. The preparation of the pupil in the Wisdom School was therefore directed primarily to the will, in order that he might grow strong enough to endure, beyond the Threshold, that picture of the world for which a highly developed consciousness of self is required.

"We see, then, what it was men feared in olden times for the pupil who was to be guided into the inner-being of the things of the world, into the inner-being of Nature. They were afraid lest he be hurt in his soul, through falling into a condition of uncertainty and darkness, a condition comparable, in the realm of soul, with physical faintness. This danger they hoped to avoid by a thoroughgoing discipline of the will. In ordinary life, they said, man must remain on this side of the realm where the dangerous knowledge is to be found; a Guardian holds him back from the region for which he is unfit, thus protecting him from being overcome by faintness of soul. And their description of the experiences the pupil had to undergo if he wanted to cross the Threshold and pass the Guardian corresponds exactly to inner experiences of the soul.

"It was told how, when the pupil draws near the Threshold, he immediately has a feeling of uncertainty. If he has been sufficiently prepared, he is able to stand upright in the realm which would otherwise make him giddy; he passes the Guardian of the Threshold and, by virtue of the powers of his soul, enters into the spiritual world—which the Guardian would otherwise not allow him even to behold. But he must be able also to stay in the spiritual world with full consciousness. For the tremendous experiences that await him there call for strength and not for weakness, and if he were to let go, these experiences would have a shattering effect on his whole organization; he would suffer grievous harm.

"And now the strange thing is that in the course of evolution a knowledge that could be attained by pupils of the ancient Wisdom Schools only after most careful preparation has become the common property of all mankind. We stand today in our ordinary knowledge beyond what the men of old felt to be a Threshold. The purpose they had in view in the ancient Wisdom Schools was that the pupil, when he looked into his own inner-being, should feel himself united there with the inner-being of Nature. And believing that if he did so unprepared, he would sink into a kind of spiritual faintness, they would not allow him to attempt this exploration until he had received the right discipline and training. And yet in our age everyone penetrates into this region utterly unprepared!

"As a matter of fact, man is experiencing today precisely what the ancients took such care to avoid. He acquires his knowledge of Nature; and he acquires also a strong consciousness of self that enables him to stand upright amid all the knowledge that is current today in astronomy, physics, chemistry, biology, etc. He imbibes this knowledge and can remain steadfast without losing his balance. Nevertheless, there is a quality in his life of soul that the men of old would deeply deplore. Because in the course of evolution we have acquired thought and the feeling of freedom and a stronger self-consciousness, therefore we do not lose ourselves when we study the results of natural science; but we do lose something, and the loss is only too manifest today in the soul-life of mankind everywhere.

"In this matter we labor under great illusion; we dream, and we cling to our dreams, and will not let them go. I have often spoken of how natural science brings conscientious students to a recognition of the boundaries of knowledge, boundaries man cannot pass without taking his power of cognition into forbidden—*nay, into impossible*—regions...

"...Out of an instinctive feeling that was conscious and yet at the same time unconscious, Goethe rejected utterly the separation of the being of man's soul from the innermost being of Nature. He saw clearly that if the soul becomes conscious, in a healthy manner, of its own real being, then that consciousness brings with it the experience of standing within the innermost heart of Nature.

"This conviction it was that kept Goethe from accepting Kant's philosophy. They make a great mistake who assert that at

our Ego-consciousness; of being so surrounded and overborne by purely mathematical pictures of the world, purely atomistic conceptions, that we lose all sense of the 'whole' world in its infinite variety and richness. In order that we may find the world again—in order, that is, that we may find the spirit in the world—we must cross what constitutes for modern man the Threshold.

"We may even put it this way: if the men of olden times feared the Guardian of the Threshold and needed to be fully prepared before they might pass him, we in our day must desire earnestly to pass the Guardian. We must long to carry knowledge of the spirit into those regions where hitherto we have relied only on external sense-perception in combination with the results of intellectual reasoning and experiment. Knowledge of the spirit must be taken into the laboratory, into the observatory and into the clinic. Wherever research is carried on, knowledge of the spirit must have a place.

"Otherwise, since all the results that are arrived at in such institutions come from beyond the Threshold, man is thereby cut off from the world in a manner that is dangerous for him. He feels himself in the presence of an inner-being of Nature which he can never approach on an external path, which he can approach only by becoming awake in his soul and pressing forward to the immortal part of his own being. As soon, however, as he does this, he is at that moment also within the spirit of Nature. He has stepped across the Threshold that lies in his own being and finds himself in the presence of the spiritual in Nature.

"To point out to man this path is the task of Anthroposophical Spiritual Science. It has to give what the other sciences cannot give. And it may rightly claim to be Goethean; for to those who say:

To Nature's heart
No living soul can reach.

Goethe replies:

Nature is neither kernel nor shell,
She is both in one, she is one and all.
Look in your own heart, man, and tell
If you yourself are kernel or shell!

"We are but a 'shell' as long as we remain in the life of ideas alone. When we sever ourselves from Nature, all we can do is to talk about her. But the man who penetrates to his own inner 'kernel,' and experiences himself in the very center of his soul—he discovers that he is at the same time in the very innermost of Nature; he is experiencing her inner-being...

"One who carries deeply enough in his heart the development of Spiritual Science will find himself continually face-to-face with this question of the connection between the being-of-man and the inner-being of Nature. The specialized sciences cannot help us here; they only spread darkness over the world. *The darkness is to be feared*, even as the men of olden times feared the region beyond the Threshold. But it is possible for man to kindle a light that shall light up the darkness—*and this light is the light that shines in the soul of man when he attains to spiritual knowledge.*"

Rudolf Steiner's
Knowledge of the
Higher Worlds

We must, in our time, initiate ourselves and not expect a Mystery initiation center (school) to take us through the training and ordeals, because they are no longer valid in our time. We must seek direct spiritual experience through the many helpers who wish to commune with us from across the threshold of the spiritual world. Once the aspirant has found a Language of Spirit to communicate with the hierarchy of spiritual beings found in Spirit-Land, a continuous stream of spiritual nutrition feeds the aspirant until they become an initiate who has been initiated by spiritual beings offering to midwife the soul into the Spirit-Self (Higher-Self). There is no better training in this process of initiation than that which is to be found in Rudolf Steiner's book, *Knowledge of the Higher Worlds and its Attainment*. In this book, Steiner addresses the question of the guardian of the threshold in a comprehensive fashion, perhaps more thoroughly than any other theosophical or theological writer.

As always, the very best way is to let Rudolf Steiner explain this in his own words. To accomplish this purpose, we include the complete Ninth Chapter of *Knowledge of the Higher Worlds* as it is the primary source within Spiritual Science on this subject. Therefore, as always in this series, it won't be surrounded by the usual quotation marks; but rather, it will be preceded and followed by a triangle.

$$\Delta$$

Knowledge of the Higher Worlds, **Rudolf Steiner, Chapter X,**
The Guardian of the Threshold, **1918, GA 10**

The important experiences marking the student's ascent into
the higher worlds include his meeting with the *Guardian of the
Threshold*. Strictly speaking, there are two *Guardians*: a *lesser*
and a *greater*. The student meets the lesser Guardian when the
threads connecting willing, feeling, and thinking within the finer
astral and etheric bodies begin to loosen, in the way described
in the foregoing chapter. The greater Guardian is encountered
when this sundering of the connections extends to the physical
parts of the body, that is, at first to the brain. The lesser Guardian
is a sovereign being. He does not come into existence, as far
as the student is concerned, until the latter has reached the
requisite stage of development. Only some of his most important
characteristics can here be indicated.

    The attempt will now be made to describe in narrative form
this meeting with the lesser Guardian of the Threshold, as a result
of which the student learns that his thinking, feeling, and willing
have become released within him from their inherent connection.

    A truly terrible spectral being confronts him, and he will
need all the presence of mind and faith in the security of his path
which he has had ample opportunity to acquire in the course of
his previous training.

    The Guardian proclaims his signification somewhat in the
following words:—

    'Hitherto, powers invisible to you watched over you. They saw
to it that in the course of your lives each of your good deeds

brought its reward, and each of your evil deeds was attended by its evil results. Thanks to their influence your character formed itself out of your life-experiences and thoughts. They were the instruments of your destiny. They ordained that measure of joy and pain allotted to you in your incarnations, according to your conduct in lives gone by. They ruled over you as the all-embracing law of *karma*. These powers will now partly release you from their constraining influence; and henceforth must you accomplish for yourself a part of the work which hitherto they performed for you. Destiny struck you many a hard blow in the past. You knew not why. Each blow was the consequence of a harmful deed in a bygone lie. You found both joy and gladness, and you accepted them as they came. For they too, were the fruits of former deeds. Your character shows both many a beautiful side, and many an ugly flaw. You have yourself to thank for both; for they are the result of your previous experiences and thoughts. Until now, these were unknown to you; as their effects alone were made manifest. The karmic powers, however, beheld all your deeds in former lives, and all your most secret thoughts and feelings, and determined accordingly your present self and your present mode of life. But now all the good and evil sides of your bygone lives shall be revealed to you. Hitherto they were interwoven with your own being; they were in you and you couldn't see them, even as you can't behold your own brain with physical eyes. But now they become released from you; they detach themselves from your personality. They assume an independent form which you can't see even as you behold the stones and plants of the outer world. And . . . I am that very being who shaped my body out of you good and evil achievements. My spectral form is woven out of your own life's record. Until now, you have borne me invisibly within you, and it was well that this was so; for the wisdom of your destiny, though concealed from you, could thus work within you, so that the hideous stains on my form should be blotted out. Now that I have come forth from within you, that concealed wisdom, too, has departed from you. It will pay no further heed to you; it will leave the work in your hands alone. I must become a perfect and glorious being, or fall prey to corruption; and should this occur, I would also drag you down with me into a dark and corrupt world. If you would avoid this, then your own wisdom must become great enough to undertake the task of that other, concealed wisdom, which has departed from you. As a form visible to yourself I will never for an instant leave your side, once you have crossed my Threshold. And in the future, whenever you act or think wrongly you will straightway perceive your guilt as a hideous, demoniacal distortion of my form. Only when you have made good all your bygone wrongs and have so purified yourself that all further evil is, for you, a thing impossible, only then will my being have become transformed into radiant beauty. Then, too, shall I again become united with you for the welfare of your future activity.

'Yet my Threshold is fashioned out of all the timidity that remains in you, out of all the dread of the strength needed to take full responsibility for all your thoughts and actions. As long as there remains in you a trace of fear of becoming by yourself the guide of your own destiny, just so long will this Threshold lack what still remains to be built into it. And as long as a single stone is found missing, just so long must you remain standing as though transfixed; or else stumble. Therefore, seek not to cross this Threshold until you feel yourself entirely free from fear and ready for the highest responsibility. Until now I only emerged from your personality when death recalled you from an earthly life; but even then my form was veiled from you. Only the powers of destiny who watched over you beheld me and could thus, in the intervals between death and a new birth, build in you, in accordance with my appearance, that power and capacity thanks to which you could labor in a new Earth-life at the beautifying of my form, for your welfare and progress. It was I, too, whose imperfection ever and again constrained the powers of destiny to lead you back to a new incarnation upon Earth. I was present at the hour of your death, and it was on my account that the Lords of Karma ordained your reincarnation. And it is only by thus unconsciously transforming me to complete perfection in ever recurring earthly lives that you could have escaped the powers of death and passed over into immortality united with me.

'I stand before you today visible, just as I have ever stood invisible beside you in the hour of death. When you shall have crossed my Threshold, you will enter those realms to which you have, until now, only had access to after physical death. You now enter them with full knowledge; and henceforth as you wander outwardly visible upon the Earth you will at the same time wander in the kingdom of death, that is—*within the kingdom of life eternal.* For I am indeed the Angel of Death—*but I am at the same time the bearer of a higher life without end.* Through me you will 'die' with your body still living—*to be reborn into an imperishable existence.*

'Into this kingdom you are now entering; you will meet beings that are supersensible—*and happiness will be your lot*. But I myself must provide your first acquaintance with that world, and I am your own creation. Formerly I drew my life from you; but now you have awakened me to a separate existence so that I stand before you as the visible gauge of your future deeds—*perhaps, too, as your constant reproach. For you have formed me—but by so doing, as your duty you have undertaken to transform me.'*

(It will be gathered from the above that the Guardian of the Threshold is an (astral) figure, revealing itself to the student's awakened higher sight; and it is to this supersensible encounter that Spiritual Science conducts him. It is a lower magical process to make the Guardian of the Threshold physically visible also. That was attained by producing a cloud of fine substance, a kind of frankincense resulting from a particular mixture of a number of substances. The developed power of the magician is then able to mold the frankincense into shape, animating it with the still unredeemed karma of the individual. Such physical phenomena are no longer necessary for those sufficiently prepared for the higher sight; and besides this, anyone who sees, without adequate preparation, his unredeemed karma appear before his eyes as a living creature would run the risk of straying into evil byways. Bulwer Lytton's *Zanoni* contains in novel form a description of the Guardian of the Threshold.)

What is here indicated in narrative form must not be understood in the sense of an allegory, but as an experience of the highest possible reality befalling the esoteric student.

The Guardian must warn him not to go a step further unless he feels in himself the strength to fulfill the demands made in the above speech. However horrible the form assumed by the Guardian, it is only the effect of the student's own past life, his own character risen out of him into independent existence. This awakening is brought about by the separation of will, thought, and feeling. To feel for the first time that one has oneself called a spiritual being into existence is in itself an experience of deepest significance. The student's preparation must aim at enabling him to endure the terrible sight without a trace of timidity and, at the moment of the meeting, to feel his strength so increased that he can undertake fully conscious the responsibility for transforming and beautifying the Guardian.

If successful, this meeting with the Guardian results in the student's next physical death being an entirely different event from the death as he knew it formerly. He experiences death consciously by laying aside the physical body as one discards a garment that is worn out or perhaps rendered useless through a sudden rent. Thus his physical death is of special importance only for those living with him, whose perception is still restricted to the world of the senses. For them the student dies; but for himself nothing of importance is changed in his whole environment. The entire supersensible world stood open to him before his death, and it is this same world that now confronts him after death.

The Guardian of the Threshold is also connected with other matters. The person belongs to a family, a nation, a race; his activity in this world depends upon his belonging to some such community. His individual character is also connected with it. The conscious activity of individual persons by no means exhausts everything to be reckoned with in a family, a nation, or a race. Besides their character, families, nations, and races have also their destiny. For persons restricted to their senses these things remain mere general ideas; and the materialistic thinker, in his prejudice, will look down with contempt on the spiritual scientist when he hears that for him, family and national character, lineal or racial destiny, are vested in beings just as real as the personality in which the character and destiny of the individual man are vested. The spiritual scientist becomes acquainted with higher worlds of which the separate personalities are members, just as arms and legs are members of the human being. Besides the separate individuals, a very real family and national group soul and racial spirit is at work in the life of a family, a people, or a race. Indeed, in a certain sense the separate individuals are merely the executive organs of these family group souls, racial spirits, and so on. It is nothing but the truth to say, for instance, that a national group soul makes use of each individual man belonging to that nation for the execution of some work. The group soul of a people does not descend into physical reality but dwells in the higher worlds and, in order to work in the physical world, makes use of the physical organs of each individual human being. In a higher sense, it is like an architect making use of workmen for executing the details of a building. In the truest sense, everyone receives his allotted task from his family, national, or racial group soul. Now, the ordinary person is by no means initiated into the higher design of his work. He joins unconsciously in the tasks of his people and of his race. From the moment the student meets the Guardian, he must not only know his own tasks, but must knowingly collaborate in those of his folk, his race. Every extension of his horizon necessarily enlarges the scope of his duties. What actually happens is that the student adds a new body to his finer soul-body. He puts on a second garment. Hitherto he found his way through the world with the coverings enveloping his personality; and what he had to accomplish for his community, his nation, his race, was directed by higher spirits who made use of his personality.

And now, a further revelation made to him by the Guardian of the Threshold is that henceforth these spirits will withdraw their guiding hand from him. He must step out of the circle of his community. Yet as an isolated personality he would become hardened in himself and decline into ruin, did he not, himself, acquire those powers which are vested in the national and racial spirits. Many, no doubt, will say: "Oh, I have entirely freed myself from all lineal and racial connections; I only want to be a human being and nothing but a human being." To these one must reply: "Who, then, brought you to this freedom? Was it not your family who placed you in the world where you now stand? Have you not your lineage, your nation, your race to thank for being what you are? They have brought you up. And if now, exalted above all prejudices, you are one of the light-bringers and benefactors of your stock and even of your race, it is to their up-bringing that you owe it. Yes, even when you say you are nothing but a human being, even the fact that you have become such a personality you owe to the spirits of your communities." Only the esoteric student learns what it means to be entirely cut off from his family, national, or racial spirit. He alone realizes, through personal experience, the insignificance of all such education in respect of the life now confronting him. For everything inculcated by education completely melts away when the threads binding will, thought, and feeling are severed. He looks back on the result of all his previous education as he might on a house crumbling away brick by brick, which he must now rebuild in a new form. And again, it is more than a mere symbolical expression to say that when the Guardian has enunciated his first statement, there arises from the spot where he stands a whirlwind which extinguishes all those spiritual lights that have hitherto illumined the pathway of his life. Utter darkness, relieved only by the rays issuing from the Guardian himself, unfolds before the student. And out of this darkness resounds the Guardian's further admonition: "Step not across my Threshold until thou dost clearly realize that thou wilt thyself illumine the darkness ahead of thee; take not a single step forward until thou art positive that thou hast sufficient oil in thine own lamp. The lamps of the guides whom thou hast hitherto followed will now no longer be available to thee." At these words, the student must turn and glance backward. The Guardian of the Threshold now draws aside a veil which till now had concealed deep life-mysteries. The family, national, and racial spirits are revealed to the student in their full activity, so that he perceives clearly on the one hand, how he has hitherto been led, and no less clearly on the other hand, that he will henceforward no longer enjoy this guidance. That is the second warning received at the Threshold from its Guardian.

Without preparation, no one could endure the sight of what has here been indicated. But the higher training which makes it possible at all for the student to advance up to the Threshold simultaneously puts him in a position to find the necessary strength at the right moment. Indeed, the training can be so harmonious in its nature that the entry into the higher life is relieved of everything of an agitating or tumultuous character. His experience at the Threshold will then be attended by a premonition of that felicity which is to provide the keynote of his newly awakened life. The feeling of a new freedom will outweigh all other feelings; and attended by this feeling, his new duties and responsibilities will appear as something which man, at a particular stage of life, must needs take upon himself.

Δ

Rudolf Steiner on the Guardian of the Threshold

A true initiate knows that the Guardian of the Threshold is, in fact, a part of his own nature. We help create the Guardian and it is the Guardian who helps us see, resolve, and discard the lower elements of our being. The Guardian should become our friend and guide as his horrifying visage becomes a familiar aid in self-knowledge that transforms and beautifies us as our Spiritual Soul gleans the eternal seeds of this world and brings them as offerings to the spiritual world. But first, we must pay the piper, give Charon his coin, tame the three-headed dog Cerberus and understand that the food and drink of the underworld, and the nectar and ambrosia of the spiritual world are completely different. Once we can gather the eternal seeds from the virtues of love, compassion, generosity, selflessness, truth, beauty, and goodness from the physical world, we will have the proper offerings that will gain access to the spiritual world beyond the Guardian.

Knowledge of Higher Worlds and its Attainment, **Rudolf Steiner,** *Life and Death: The Greater Guardian of the Threshold,* **1918, GA 10**

"It has been described how significant for the human being is his meeting with the so-called lesser Guardian of the Threshold by virtue of the fact that he becomes aware of confronting a supersensible being whom he has himself brought into existence, and whose body consists of the hitherto invisible results of the student's own actions, feelings, and thoughts. These unseen forces have become the cause of his destiny and his character, and he realizes how he himself founded the present in the past. He can understand why his inner-self, now standing to a certain extent revealed before him, includes particular inclinations and habits, and he can also recognize the origin of certain blows of fate that have befallen him. He perceives why he loves one thing and hates another; why one thing makes him happy and another unhappy. Visible life is explained by the invisible causes. The essential facts of life, too—health and illness, birth and death—unveil themselves before his gaze. He observes how before his birth he wove the causes which necessarily led to his return to life. Henceforth he knows that being within himself, which is fashioned with all its imperfections in the visible world, and which can only be brought to its final perfection in this same visible world. For in no other world is an opportunity given to build up and complete this being. Moreover, he recognizes that death cannot sever him forever from this world…

"Thanks to his insight into the supersensible world, the initiate gains a better knowledge and appreciation of the true value of visible nature than was possible before his higher training; and this may be counted among his most important experiences. Anyone not possessing this insight and perhaps therefore imagining the supersensible regions to be infinitely more valuable, is likely to underestimate the physical world. Yet the possessor of this insight knows that without experience in visible reality he would be totally powerless in that other invisible reality. Before he can live in the latter he must have the requisite faculties and instruments which can only be acquired in the visible world. Consciousness in the invisible world is not possible without spiritual sight, but this power of vision in the higher world is gradually developed through experience in the lower. No one can be born in the spiritual world with spiritual eyes without having first developed them in the physical world, any more than a child could be born with physical eyes, had they not already been formed within the mother's womb.

"From this standpoint it will also be readily understood why the Threshold to the supersensible world is watched over by a Guardian. In no case may real insight into those regions be permitted to anyone lacking the requisite faculties; therefore, when at the hour of death anyone enters the other world while still incompetent to work in it, the higher experiences are shrouded from him until he is fit to behold them…

"Thus, the first Guardian confronts man as the counterpart of his two-fold nature in which perishable and imperishable are blended; and it stands clearly proved how far removed he still is from attaining that sublime luminous figure which may again dwell in the pure, spiritual world. The extent to which he is entangled in the physical sense-world is exposed to the student's view. The presence of instincts, impulses, desires, egotistical wishes and all forms of selfishness, and so forth, expresses itself in this entanglement, as it does further in his membership in a race, a nation, and so forth; for peoples and races are but steps leading to pure humanity…

"When the student has recognized all the elements from which he must liberate himself, his way is barred by a sublime luminous being whose beauty is difficult to describe in the words of human language. This encounter takes place when the sundering of the organs of thinking, feeling, and willing extends to the physical body, so that their reciprocal connection is no longer regulated by themselves but by the higher consciousness, which has now entirely liberated itself from physical conditions. The organs of thinking, feeling, and willing shall then be controlled from supersensible regions as instruments in the power of the human soul. The latter, thus liberated from all physical bonds, is now confronted by the second Guardian of the Threshold who speaks as follows:—

'You have released yourself from the world of the senses. You have won the right to become a citizen of the supersensible world, where your activity can now be directed. For your own sake, you no longer require the physical body in its present form. If your intention was merely to acquire the faculties necessary for life in the supersensible world, you need no longer return to the sense-world. But now behold me. See how sublimely I tower above all that you have made of yourself thus far. You have attained thy present degree of perfection thanks to the faculties you were able to develop in the sense-world as long as you were still confined to it. But now a new era is to begin, in which your liberated powers must be applied to further work in the world of the senses. Until now, you have sought only your own release; but now, having yourself become free, you can go forth as a liberator of your companions. For until today you have striven as an individual; but now seek to coordinate yourself with the whole, so that you may bring into the supersensible world not only yourself, but everything that exists in the world of the senses. You will someday be able to unite with me; but I cannot receive blessing so long as others remain unredeemed. As a separate freed being, you would gladly enter at once the kingdom of the supersensible; yet you would be forced to look down on the remaining unredeemed beings in the physical world—having separated your destiny from theirs—*although you and they are inseparably united.* For you all did necessarily descend into the sense-world in order to gather the powers needed for a higher world. To separate yourself from your companions would be an abuse of those very powers which you could not have developed except in their company. You couldn't have descended, had they not done so; and so, without them the powers needed for supersensible existence would fail you. For you must now share with your companions the powers which, you acquired along with them. I shall therefore bar you entry into the higher regions of the supersensible world so long as you have not applied all the powers you have acquired to the liberation of your companions. With the powers already at your disposal you may journey in the lower regions of the supersensible world; but I stand before the portal of the higher regions as the Cherub with the fiery sword before Paradise, and I bar your entrance as long as powers unused in the sense-world still remain in you. And if you refuse to apply your powers in this world, others will come who will not refuse; and a higher supersensible world will receive all the fruits of the sense-world, while you will lose from under your feet the very ground in which thou were rooted. The purified world will develop above and beyond you, and you shall be excluded from it. For thereby you wouldst tread the *black path*, while the others from whom you severed yourself tread the *white path.*'

"With these words the greater Guardian makes his presence known soon after the meeting with the first Guardian has taken place. The initiate knows full well what is in store for him if he yields to the temptation of a premature abode in the supersensible world. An indescribable splendor shines forth from the second Guardian of the Threshold; union with him looms as a far distant ideal before the soul's vision. Yet there is also the certitude that this union will not be possible until all the powers afforded by this world are applied to the task of its liberation and redemption. By fulfilling the demands of the higher light-being the initiate will contribute to the liberation of the human race. He lays his gifts on the sacrificial altar of humanity. Should he prefer his own premature elevation into the supersensible world, the stream of human evolution will flow over and past him. After his liberation he can gain no new powers from the world of the senses; and if he places his work at the world's disposal it will entail his renouncement of any further benefit for himself.

"It does not follow that, when called upon to decide, anyone will naturally follow the white path. That depends entirely upon whether he is so far purified at the time of his decision that no trace of self-seeking makes this prospect of felicity appear desirable. For the allurements here are the strongest possible; whereas on the other side no special allurements are evident. Here nothing appeals to his egotism. The gift he receives in the higher regions of the supersensible world is nothing that comes to him—but only something that flows from him, that is, *love for the world and for his companions*. Nothing that egotism desires is denied upon the black path; for the latter provides, on the contrary, for the complete gratification of egotism, and will not fail to attract those desiring merely their own felicity—*for it is indeed the appropriate path for them*. No one therefore should expect the occultists of the white path to give him instruction for the development of his own egotistical self. They do not take the slightest interest in the felicity of the individual man. Each can attain that for himself, and it is not the task of the white occultists to shorten the way; for they are only concerned with the development and liberation of all human beings and all creatures. Their instructions therefore deal only with the development of powers for collaboration in this work. Thus they place selfless devotion and self-sacrifice before all other qualities. They never actually refuse anyone—*for even the greatest egotist can purify himself*; but no one merely seeking an advantage for himself will ever obtain assistance from the white occultists. Even when they do not refuse their help, he, the seeker, deprives himself on the advantage resulting from their assistance. Anyone, therefore, really following the instructions of the good occultists will, upon crossing the Threshold, understand the demands of the greater Guardian; anyone, however, not following their instructions can never hope to reach the Threshold. Their instructions, if followed, produce good results or no results; for it is no part of their task to lead to egotistical felicity and a mere existence in the supersensible worlds. In fact, it becomes their duty to keep the student away from the supersensible world until he can enter it with the will for selfless collaboration."

Lectures to the First Class, **Volume II, Rudolf Steiner, Lesson XIV, Dornach, May 31, 1924, GA 270**

"We have been considering the human being's relation to the Guardian of the Threshold and have led our souls step-by-step to see what our relation is to the Guardian of the Threshold on the path of knowledge. Today we intend to enliven the situation of standing before the Guardian in order to advance a step further in this esoteric consideration.

"I will repeat what has been considered in the previous lessons regarding this situation. Man leaves the physical world in which he develops his normal consciousness. He realizes that although this sensible-physical world can be wonderful, joyful as well as painful and full of suffering, it can also be majestic—and that he has every reason to consciously be a part of it. But he also realizes that he can never know himself if he merely directs his attention and his feelings to this physical world. He must say to himself: As wonderful as it is, with all its amazing variety of colors and forms, what I myself am, what my origin and being are, cannot be found in the scope of this environment.

"Nevertheless, from all sides the words resound as the most important task in the life of the human being: O man, know thyself!

"And it also becomes clear that in normal life we are protected from entering unprepared into the world which is the world of his real being. And the Guardian of the Threshold is the one who protects us from consciously perceiving his environment when we are sleeping at night; for what we would then perceive, unprepared, would be such a terrible shock that we would not be able to lead a normal human waking life.

"The Guardian of the Threshold also makes it clear to us that he—the Guardian of the Threshold—is the true, the real gateway to the spiritual world.

"Thus, the person realizes that before he enters the kingdom of knowledge he comes to an abyss, which at first seems bottomless. The support of the physical world ends here. He cannot cross it. One can only cross this abyss by freeing oneself from the physical, when one—symbolically speaking—'grows wings,' in order to cross the abyss as a psychic-spiritual being.

"But the Guardian of the Threshold calls forth to him to beware of the abyss, especially to be aware of the beasts which rise up as spiritual figures from this abyss, that one should realize that these beasts are the outer reflections of impure willing, feeling and thinking—that they first must be overcome. And in a graphic image one sees how his willing, feeling, and thinking appear in three animals—one ghastly, one horrid to look at, and so forth.

"Then, the Guardian of the Threshold shows us how thinking, feeling, and willing can strengthen themselves after having consciously determined to overcome the beasts. To enter the spiritual world, to visualize the spiritual world, we need to develop situation-meditations in order to feel how the Cosmos speaks to us, how the hierarchies speak to us, how at first everything foretells what awaits us there in the spiritual world.

"And from what has entered our souls through the mantras, we will realize ever more that the human being must become different when he crosses the abyss, when he wishes to live into what is beyond the abyss. We will realize ever more: Here on Earth, we associate with the beings of the three nature kingdoms and with men; beyond we associate with disembodied souls and with the spirits of the higher hierarchies. It is a different kind of relating, which requires a different state of mind. [original: *Seelenverfassung* = soul-constitution]

"It is again the task of the Guardian of the Threshold to strongly indicate how the human being must comport himself when faced with the fact that when he crosses the abyss and experiences something of the reality of the spiritual world, he must do so with a completely different state of mind.

"The person will realize that two states of mind can be a reality within him: the one on this side of the abyss with normal consciousness; and the one beyond the abyss, outside the physical and etheric bodies—the state of mind in the purely spiritual world.

"When the difference between these states of mind appears, great dangers await him, dangers which appear at first to be slight deviations from the normal state of mind which are always present within the psyche, but which are pathological deformities when carried to an extreme. Of course it must be emphasized: When the journey to the higher worlds is undertaken as it is carefully described in my book *Knowledge of the Higher Worlds and its Attainment,* in many shorter works which have appeared in anthroposophical circles, and in the second part of my *An Outline Of Occult Science,* then aberration from the normal condition of the mind cannot occur, not even in the slightest degree. The person will cross into the spiritual world in the full consciousness of normal human understanding, first in knowledge and also through initiation. But he must know how, in two ways, he may lose the everyday capacity for understanding, which holds him securely to life, if he does not adhere to the right guidelines into the spiritual world.

"Here on this side of the threshold we are standing on the Earth, on the solid earthly elements. The ground is beneath our feet, it is our support. Around us is the watery element; which also participates in the formation of our own bodies. In ordinary life this watery element cannot support us, but it interpenetrates us, transforms itself into our blood. It is contained in our growth, in our forces of nutrition. We breathe the air. The airy or gaseous element is all around us. Warmth is all around us: the warmth ether, the fourth element.

"In ordinary life they are separate from each other. Where there is solid earth there is not water; where there is water there is not air; where there is air there is not water. Only fire—warmth— interpenetrates all. It is the only thing which interpenetrates everything.

"The moment we leave the physical body—also with the first push, my dear friends—this separation of the elements ceases. We enlarge ourselves, we expand, and at the same time we are in earth, water, fire, air. We can no longer distinguish them from each other and the individual attributes of these four elements have ceased to exist. The earth is no longer our support, for it is no longer solid. The water no longer forms us, for its formative force has ended. Once in the spiritual world it is as though we were dissolving, as ice melts in warm water; for we have become one with the water. We could not float in it; for that would mean that we were still separate from it. The blood is no longer a separate element in the blood vessels; but our blood becomes one with the all-pervading watery element of the Universe. And air: it ceases being the formative breathing force in us. Warmth ceases to enkindle us to an 'I,' and make us feel that we are a Self within the warmth. It all ends. We must meet this ending of the differentiation between earth, water, air and fire in the right frame of mind.

"Imagine that we have already flown over the abyss. We have arrived on the other side, my dear sisters and brothers. The Guardian of the Threshold calls out to us, we should turn around again and face him.

"Imagine it vividly, my dear sisters and brothers. The person has arrived on the other side, where the truths and knowledge of the spirit will be revealed to him. He stands on the other side. The Guardian of the Threshold invokes him to turn around in order to receive the advice he needs now that he has been touched by the state-of-mind, which is on the other side of the threshold, where one lives within the four elements: in earth, water, air, fire.

"He encounters there—pardon the trivial expression, my dear sisters and brothers—the illusion of being in love with the release from the solid earth, from the formative water force, from the creative force of air, from the selfhood awakening force of warmth; he feels delight in spiritual beatitude, dedicated to it and wishes to remain in this state of spiritual beatitude. It overcomes him because the luciferic temptation is approaching him. Depending on his karma, he can be more or less susceptible to this temptation. If he is so susceptible that he is utterly in love with the experience of dissolving into earth, water, air, and fire, the luciferic forces will apprehend him and he will no longer leave this state-of-mind. He succumbs to the danger of continuing in this state of mind when he returns to everyday life.

"The Guardian of the Threshold must call out to him: You may not do that. You may not succumb to Lucifer. You may not merely feel the delight of bliss in dissolving in earth, water, fire, air. When you return to the physical world you must again take on the state of mind of ordinary consciousness; otherwise in the future you will be an unstable person in the physical world.

"That is the luciferic danger, that upon return from the spiritual world, from beyond the threshold, one becomes an unstable, confused person, no longer versed in the ways of the world, a dreamer who confuses dreaming for idealism and who is contemptuous of ordinary consciousness. That you must not do. And the Guardian of the Threshold urgently admonishes us that we must resolve to live in the world, be it the Earthly, be it the spiritual, in the way which corresponds to each.

"But the Guardian of the Threshold adds a second admonishment: that when we cross over with separated thinking, feeling and willing, we must pay attention to what extent Earthly inclinations are still present in this thinking, feeling and willing.

"The person may be inclined to fixate on his experiences on this side of the threshold because of having the Earth's support and cross the threshold in a materialistic state-of-mind, cross with the congealed formative forces of water. If so, he can be plagued by earthly arrogance and say to himself: In life on Earth I breathed, inhaled that breath from which the Father-God once created the human soul, human life. I can also do that if only I am freed from Earthly limitations.

"But if the person wants to bring over into the spiritual world what he has of creative divine force through his breath, he will succumb to the ahrimanic temptation. Then, he will not be able to return; because before he does so he will become faint. He will be more or less unconscious. His consciousness will be paralyzed. Because his consciousness has been paralyzed, he more or less becomes an instrument of the ahrimanic powers in the spiritual world.

"Although today humanity is crudely hardened by materialism, since the beginning of the Michael Age, it is almost being dragged over into the spiritual world by spiritual life itself. And what it means when the ahrimanic powers seize humanity when its consciousness is paralyzed, though otherwise in a fully waking state, has been amply demonstrated, my dear friends, by the outbreak of the great [first] World War.

"When this World War broke out, I said to many people: The history of this war cannot be written from the physical plane alone. Documents alone do not speak the truth, because of the thirty or forty men in Europe who directly participated in the outbreak of the war, many of them had dimmed consciousness at the decisive moments. They became instruments for the ahrimanic powers on this side. So that much of what happened during this war was instigated by the ahrimanic powers. The war can only be written about in an occult way.

"What is seen—in many respects modified on this side of the threshold—in many leading personalities at the outbreak of this World War, can be observed in those who preserved the habits of the mind and carried them over beyond the threshold and whose consciousness became paralyzed, muted, and they became instruments of the ahrimanic powers.

"It must be perfectly clear that the human being may not carry over to this side the state-of-mind applicable to beyond the threshold, and that he may not carry over to the other side the state-of-mind applicable to this side. Rather must he develop a strong inner human consciousness for each domain—for this side and also for beyond the threshold."

The Evolution of Consciousness, **Rudolf Steiner, Lecture V,**
The Relation of Man to the Three Worlds, **August 23, 1923, GA 227**

"But look—with really flexible thinking, free from prejudice, you will be able to keep up. And for anyone who thinks in this way, with healthy human understanding, there is a certain consolation. As I said before, the actual thrusting aside of the veil of chaos and the entry into the threefold world, which sends its activity and substance into the physical world in so vastly complicated a way—this experience is so bewildering that full warning of it is given before the threshold is crossed. I will put it pictorially, but in full accord with the facts. The warning is:—

'If you are not willing to forgo what you have regarded as ordinary naturalistic logic and as the customary connections between things, if you are reluctant to leave behind this physical cloak, it is better that you should not enter the spiritual world, for there you will be obliged to make use of other associations of ideas, other orderings, and a completely different logic. If you want to take anything of your physical logic with you into the spiritual world, you will quite certainly get confused.'

"And among the matters that have to do with preparing ourselves for meditation and concentration, we have to remember the warning never to carry over the logic of the sense-world into the logic of the spiritual world.

"This is the important warning given by that power we may call the Guardian of the Threshold—of whom we shall hear more in later lectures—to those who wish to pierce behind the veil.

"But when we wish to return to the physical world, we receive from the Guardian another warning, clear and forcible. So long as we are men of Earth we return, or we should never get away from happenings in the spiritual world, and our deserted physical body would die. We must always return. Pay heed to the second warning given by the Guardian who stands where the veil of chaos separates the physical sense-world from the spiritual world. This, then, is the warning:—

'During your life on Earth, never for a moment forget that you have been in the spiritual world; then and only then, during the times you have to spend in the physical world, will you be able to guide your steps with certainty.'

"Thus, at the threshold of this threefold spiritual world, to which a man is related through his three members in the way described, he is warned to lay aside all naturalistic logic, to leave behind this cloak of the senses and to go forward prepared to adapt himself to a spiritual logic, spiritual thinking and the spiritual association of ideas. On his return he is given a second warning, just as stern, even sterner than the first: never for a moment to forget his experience in the spiritual world—in other words, not to confine himself in ordinary consciousness merely to the impulses of the sense-world, and so on; but always to be conscious that to his physical world he has to be a bearer of the spiritual.

"You will see that the two warnings differ considerably from one another. At the entrance to the spiritual world the Guardian of the Threshold says:—

'Forget the physical world of the senses while here you are acquiring knowledge of the spiritual. But on your return to the physical world the Guardian's warning is: Never forget, even in the physical world on Earth, your experiences in the heavenly world of the spirit; keep your memory of them alive.'

"...In the case of those I pictured coming to the Mystery Centers as inspired pupils, or just as ordinary folk, the transition from sleeping to waking and from waking to sleeping was not made without their being instinctively aware of the Guardian of the Threshold. Three or four thousand years ago, as men were entering sleep, there arose in their souls a dream, a picture of the Guardian. *They passed him by.* And as they were returning from sleep to ordinary life, once again this picture appeared. The warnings they received on entering and leaving the spiritual world were not so clear as the warnings which I have said are given to those entering the spiritual world through Inspiration and Imagination. But as they fell asleep, and again as they awoke, they had a dreamlike experience of passing the Guardian of the Threshold, not unlike their other instinctive perceptions of the spiritual world. Further progress in the evolution of humanity required that man should gain his freedom by losing his spiritual vision, and he had to forfeit that half-sleeping, half-waking state during which he was able to behold, at least in a kind of dream, the majestic figure of the Guardian of the Threshold.

"Nowadays, between going to sleep and waking, a man passes the Guardian but does not know it. He is blind and deaf to the Guardian, and that is why he finds himself in a dream world which is so completely disorganized.

"Now consider quite impartially the different way in which the people of older epochs knew how to speak of their dreams. Because of ignoring the Guardian every morning, every evening, and twice every time he takes an afternoon nap, a man today experiences this utter disorder and chaos in his dream-world. This can be seen in the form taken by any dream.

"Only think: when we cross the Threshold—and we do so each time we go to sleep—there stands the majestic Guardian. He cannot be ignored without everything we meet in the spiritual world becoming disordered. How this happens is best seen in the metamorphosis undergone by the orderly thinking proper to the physical, naturalistic world when this passes into the imagery of dreams. Individual dreams can show this very clearly…

"When, ignoring the Guardian, we cross the Threshold, we confront three worlds, and we can make nothing of them because we partly carry over into the world of spirit the outlook we are familiar with in the waking world. The spiritual world, however, asserts its own order to a certain extent…

"…Because of ignoring the Guardian of the Threshold, you carry over into the spiritual world a custom suited to the physical world. You connect the three worlds chaotically, according to the laws of the physical world, and you feel yourself to be in this situation.

"In countless dreams the essential thing is that when we pass the Threshold without heeding the Guardian's warning, what we perceive here in the physical, naturalistic world as a harmonious unity falls apart, and we are confronted by three different worlds. By faithfully observing the warning given by the Guardian of the Threshold, we must find the way to unite these three worlds. Today, a man in his dreams finds himself faced by these three worlds—it was not so to the same extent for anyone in older epochs, as can be seen from the dreams recorded in the *Old Testament*—and he then tries to connect the three worlds in accordance with laws valid in physical life. That is the reason for the chaotic connections in the three worlds, as they are experienced by a man of today."

The Effect of Occult Development Upon the Self and the Sheaths of Man, Rudolf Steiner, Lecture VIII, The Hague, March 27, 1913, GA 145

"As we approach the processes in the astral body and in the Self of man as experienced in occult development, it becomes more and more difficult to describe them. For the experience in these parts of human nature is far removed from the experience of everyday life. In the ordinary life of the soul we usually experience life in the astral body as the flowing and ebbing of desires, emotions, impulses, passions, etc.; and we also feel as our inward life that which is expressed collectively in the ego ['I']. But what is thus experienced is really nothing but the reflection, the mirroring of the self and the astral body in the etheric body and the physical body; it is no conscious experience of the astral body and the self. We cannot through what we experience in the ordinary life of the soul obtain a true idea of the actual experience in the higher worlds in our astral body and self; therefore, when we describe these things, we must have recourse to a kind of representation suited to these higher worlds, we must have recourse to imaginations: and these imaginations are really actually experienced. But one must not imagine that the beholding of the clairvoyant imaginations is the only thing that we experience; in a sense it is not even the principal thing; the principal thing is what we then experience inwardly through it; the processes and inward tests which the soul goes through when it confronts these imaginations.

"And this is particularly the case with such an important and powerful imagination as that which has been described as the Paradise-Imagination. One who really experiences this Paradise-Imagination, who can have it before him as a conquest in higher experience, feels himself standing in the middle of an inner surging of the soul, he feels himself laid hold of by an inner soul-wave, and he feels that he himself might err in the two different directions described in the last lecture; he feels himself attracted, vividly attracted by all the passions and emotions which continue to work from the personal life he had previously led on the physical plane; for the personal interests which we have gradually acquired on the physical plane work with ever-increasing strength as numberless magnetic forces of attraction. But, on the other hand, he feels something else. The nearer he comes, the more clearly he sees this Paradise-Imagination, the more power have these forces which draw him down to personal interests. What they bring about in him is that they blot out the Paradise-Imagination more and more, or perhaps it would be better to say that they prevent it from appearing properly; he is as though benumbed: the personal interests, emotions, feelings, sensations, etc., which we drag about with us, are so many hundreds and hundreds of magnetic forces which are so many causes of stupefaction. When the student tries to progress so far in his self-training that he observes his astral body more and more truthfully (for the Paradise-Imagination is experienced outside the physical body and etheric body, that is, in the astral body and Ego ['I']), when he has grasped the true nature and character of the astral body, he knows that it is the Egotist. And he alone is in the right position at this point, which he has reached through self-training, if he does not allow his egotistical interests to become personal to his nature and to draw him with numberless forces, but can make the interests of the whole of humanity and the world more and more his own. At this stage of occult development a counter-balance against the egotism of the astral body is felt, something which is the more evident, the more the egotistic forces bestir themselves in the now liberated astral body. There is an ever-increasing feeling of solitude, icy solitude. This icy solitude is also part of what is experienced in the inward surging of the soul. It is this icy solitude which cures one of allowing egotism to have the upper hand, and the student has trained himself correctly if at this point in his occult development he can feel the impulse to be everything through himself and for himself, and can at the same time also feel the frosty solitude approaching him.

"It is just as important to have this feeling as to approach gradually to the Paradise-Imagination. And when these two forces, that of the egotism which expands to world-interests and the frosty solitude, work together, the student then draws nearer and nearer to the Paradise-Imagination. And when this latter appears in all its vividness, when it is actually there, the time has also arrived for experiencing the meeting with the Guardian of the Threshold in the entirely right way. It is difficult to give a single description of the Guardian of the Threshold—I have done so on different occasions in our theosophical considerations. It is not so much our task today to describe the Guardian of the Threshold as to describe the inward experiences in the sheaths of man and in the human self. If the student draws closer to the Paradise-Imagination; that is to say, if it becomes more and more vivid, and he meets the Guardian of the Threshold, he then feels the full force of magnetic forces, and as he confronts the Guardian of the Threshold he feels—and this is a dreadful sensation—he feels as though chained or rooted to the spot. For all the magnetic forces which draw him down to what is personal now exercise their strongest influence; and only if he progressed to the point at which the frosty solitude has become so instructive that he is really able to make the world's interests his own, does he pass the Guardian of the Threshold; and then only does he feel himself united with the Paradise-Imagination, and become one with it. He then feels himself within it. The experience is like a coming into a right relationship with the world-interests, so that he can confess:—

'Now only may I allow my own interests to assert themselves; for they have become the interests of the world.'

"But if he does not pass, if he has not yet acquired sufficient universal interests, his personal interests then draw him back and there comes about what in Occultism is described as: *not passing the Guardian of the Threshold*. These personal interests obscure the Paradise-Imagination; he may obtain separate parts of it, as it were, indistinct impressions—*but not perfect ones*—and one is dragged back, as it were, into the personal life. It may then happen that he has thereby received the power to have a certain degree of clairvoyant experience; but these are then really maya-experiences [illusions]; they may be quite misleading, for they are entirely permeated and clouded by personal interests…

"I will suppose that the student has passed the Guardian of the Threshold and the union with the Paradise-Imagination is accomplished; that he feels within it, as if this Paradise-Imagination had now become his own greater astral sheath. He still distinctly feels his own astral body about him, and knows that it is connected with his Self, but at the same time he knows that this astral body extends its interests to all that concerns the objects and beings of the Paradise-Imagination. When the student knows his union with the Paradise-Imagination is accomplished, he may then have somewhat the following impression: he will perceive his own astral body as belonging to him, and when he has felt sufficiently what has just been described as icy solitude, this feeling becomes a power within him, and it will preserve him from gazing at nothing but himself after his accomplishment of his union with the Paradise-Imagination. He will thereby create for himself, as it were, the organ by which he may behold other beings. His occult vision will first fall on another being, a being who will make a special impression upon him, because it will appear just like himself. He himself feels that he is in his Self and astral body; the other being also at first appears to him with a Self and an astral body. This is because the qualities and powers which the pupil brings with him to such a moment enables him to see just such a being, which presents itself as if in a self and an astral body. The student will now have the following experience—produced by the frosty solitude which he has learned to bear.

The forces of his astral body will be seen endeavoring to flow outwards. If I were to represent this in diagram, I should have to draw the Self something like the nucleus of a comet, and the astral body like the comet's tail spreading out above.

"But that is only a diagram; for the student really sees a being, he sees himself as a being, and this vision is much more complex than the vision of one's own being as physical man. He also sees within his own self the other being to which he looks across. As already said, this is a typical experience. His vision simply falls upon such a being, but he feels that this being is not in such a sphere of frosty solitude as he is himself, and therefore its astral body is seen as though directed downwards. It is extremely important to experience this, to feel oneself as if in an astral body which opens upwards, develops its rays of force upwards, wishes to stream upwards, and yet to see the other being as a Self whose astral body develops its forces downwards.

"With this typical experience there now comes into the self-consciousness something like the following:— *'I am of a lower degree, of less value than this other being. What is valuable in the other being is that it can open its astral body downwards, it can, as it were, pour its forces downwards.'* And the student's impression is that of having left the physical world. The forces which proceed downwards from the astral body of the other go to the physical world, and work there as forces of blessing; in short, he has the impression that he is confronting a being that may send down to the Earth, as a Spiritual rain of blessing, that which it has acquired in the Spiritual World; whereas he himself cannot direct his astral body downwards, it insists on going upwards. He has a feeling that he is of less value; because he cannot direct his astral body downwards. Further, he has a feeling that this consciousness arising thus within him must lead to a *Spiritual Act*. A Spiritual decision matures. This Spiritual decision is to take his loneliness to this second being and warm his coldness with his warmth; he unites himself with this other being. Now, for a moment he has the impression that his own consciousness is being blotted out, as though he had brought about a sort of killing of his own being, a sort of consuming of his own being as though by fire. Then flashes into the self-consciousness, which had previously felt itself blotted out, something which he now first learns to know: Inspiration. He feels himself inspired. It is like a conversation, a typical conversation, now held with a being whom he has only learned to know because it allows him to share in its inspiration. If a student is really capable of understanding what this being sends in as his inspiring voice, he might translate what it says in somewhat the following words:— *'Because you have found the way to the other and have united yourself with his beneficial rain of sacrifice, you may*

*return to the Earth with him, within him, and I will make you
his guardian on the Earth.'* And the student has the feeling that
something of infinite importance has been taken into his soul
through being able to hear these words of inspiration. In the
Spiritual there is a being that is more precious than oneself, and
that is allowed to pour its astral being downwards in blessing.
Through the impression of being able to unite with this being,
and being its guardian when he descends, the student first learns
to understand how, as physical human beings who tread the
Earth, we are really related through our physical and etheric
coverings to that which is impregnated as higher powers in the
Self and the astral body. In our physical and etheric coverings we
are guardians of that which is to develop further and further to
higher spheres. Only in this inner-experience, when he feels his
external-being as the guardian of the inner-being, does a man
really have a true understanding of the relation of the external-
being to the inner-being of man.

"Now, when the student has passed the Guardian of the
Threshold, the experience which I have just described does
not stand alone, but is followed by another. I have described
the purely clairvoyant and inspired experience the student
may have when, outside the physical body and etheric body,
he arrives at union with the Paradise-Imagination, and then
obtains the inspiration which first gives an idea of the inter-
relationship between the sheaths. But when he has passed the
Guardian of the Threshold a second impression is added to the
first one; the vision opens past the Guardian of the Threshold
down into the physical world. I draw a line to represent the
boundary between the higher Spiritual worlds and the physical
world; above it is the realm of the Spiritual worlds and below
that of the physical.

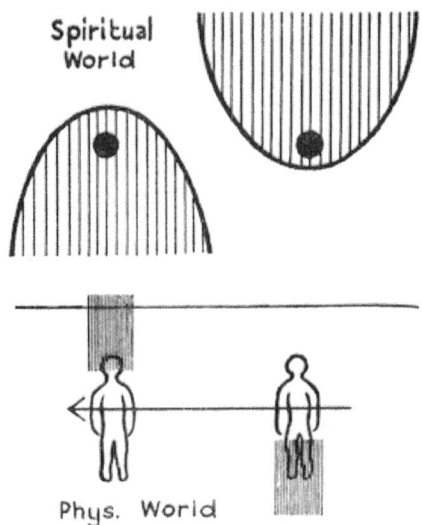

"He now sees down into the physical world, as it were, and there appears another picture, a picture of himself standing below as man. The student observes his own astral body; but this astral body which now appears as a reflection is directed downwards, it does not try to develop the force to stream towards the Spiritual World; it clings closely, as it were, to the physical plane, it does not raise itself to the heights. He also sees the reflection of the other being, whose astral body streams upwards. He has the feeling that this astral body is streaming into the Spiritual World. He sees himself and he sees the other, and he has the feeling:— *'You stand there below once more; in the place of the other being there stands there below a quite different man; he is a better man than you; his astral body strives upward, it rises upward like smoke. While your astral body strives towards the Earth, it goes like smoke downward.'* He has a feeling of the Self which dwells within him as he thus looks down, and the following dreadful impression comes to him:— *'Within thee a resolve is being formed, a dreadful resolve, the resolution to kill that other that you feel to be better than you.'*

The student knows that this decision does not come entirely from the Self; for his Self is there above. It is another being that speaks out of the one there below; but this being suggests the decision to kill the other. And he again hears the voice which previously inspired him, but now it sounds as a dreadful, avenging voice:—

'Where is thy brother?'

And from this self bursts forth a voice hostile to the former. Previously the inspiration was as follows:—

'Through having united yourself with the beneficent powers of the other being, you desire to pour yourself downwards with them, and I will make you the guardian of the other being.'

There now bursts forth from this being, that one recognizes as oneself, the words:—

'I will not be my brother's keeper.'

First comes the resolve to kill the other, then the protest against the inspiring voice which said:—

'Because you have wished to unite your coldness with that warmth I appoint you to be the guardian of that other;' the protest:— *'I will not be his guardian.'*

"When we have had this imaginative experience, we then know all of which the human soul is capable, and above all we know one thing: that, if perverted, the noblest things in the

Spiritual World may become the most dreadful things in the
physical world. We know that in the depths of the human soul,
through the perversion of the noblest readiness to sacrifice,
may arise the wish to kill our companion. From this moment
we know what is meant in the *Bible* by the story of Cain and
Abel—*but only from this moment*—for the story of Cain and Abel
is none other than the reproduction of an occult experience,
which has just been described. If the writer of the story of Cain
and Abel had been able to describe what took place with man
before the time of the story of Paradise from other reasons than
those displayed in the course of the development of humanity,
he would have described the first experience, the upper one (on
the diagram). Thus he begins with the story of Paradise, and
describes its reflection; for Cain felt in this manner towards Abel
before that period in the development of the Earth indicated by
the story of Paradise, he felt towards him as it has been shown
here above. And after the temptation, and after the loss of the
vision which is regained in occult vision through the Paradise-
Imagination, Cain's readiness to sacrifice had passed into what
appears here below; his readiness to sacrifice had really changed
into the wish to kill the other. The cry we read of in the *Bible:*—
'*Am I to be my brother's keeper?*' is the reverse reflection of the
other inspiration:— '*I will make you the guardian of the other
here below on the Earth.*' From this you will be able to see that
these typical experiences are certainly important; for they bring
about a certain union between what we may be today and the
interests common to all humanity. But at the same time they
show us very clearly by what we experience in them in our
pulsing soul-life, that the principal thing is to feel the colossal
leap the development of humanity has made from what I
described to you as the first, the pre-earthly imagination, as it

were, to that which is presented in the story of Cain and Abel as an event in humanity after the expulsion from Paradise, after the expulsion through which the Guardian of the Threshold has become invisible for man. The knowledge of this leap in the development of humanity really first shows us what this earthly man is; for when we really feel through and through what has just been described, we gradually experience that this earthly man, as he now is here upon the Earth—*is the perversion of what he once was.* And we then know with great certainty what we should have become if nothing else had intervened. If we had simply developed in this earthly evolution without anything further, we should have become aware of what this is the reflection on the Earth. We were not to know this to begin with. It is really only in our present age that man is allowed to know of what the story of Cain and Abel is the reflection, that it is the reflection of a lofty sacrifice. All that was above, everything before Paradise was concealed; for the Guardian himself hid it from us, when, in other words, man was driven out of Paradise. This could only come about through the physical body and etheric body of man being now so permeated with forces that he does not carry out what appears as the reflection—*for he certainly would carry it out if he were to feel all that is in the astral body.* The physical body and etheric body so stupefy the human being that his wish to kill his fellow is not actualized. Consider what is said in this simple sentence:— '*In that the good, progressive, divine Spiritual Powers gave man a physical and an etheric body, so that he cannot look back, something like a sort of stupefaction was at the same time poured over the wish for the war of all against all.*' The desire for this is not roused in the soul, because the physical body and etheric body of man were prepared in such a way that this desire is benumbed. A person cannot see his astral body; therefore this wish, too, remains unknown to him—*he does not carry it out.*

"If we wish really to describe the interaction of the astral body and the self, we must describe things which not only actually remain hidden to human nature—*but which must so remain.* But what has been brought about through the stunning of this and similar wishes—wishes connected with the annihilation and destruction of human and other communal life on the physical plane? They have become debilitated; the human soul only perceives them in a weakened form; it only feels them to a slight extent. And the dim feeling of those wishes that would be something so terrible if man were to allow them free expression, as they really are—*this is really our human earthly knowledge.*

"I am now giving you for the first time a definition of the nature of human earthly knowledge. It consists of the dim and dulled impulses of destruction. *Shiva [the Lord of Destruction] in his most terrible form.* That is so far stupefied that he cannot freely find expression. But is, as it were, made threadbare, compressed into the human world of ideas—this is the Maya [illusion] of the human being, this is the knowledge of man. Thus knowledge had to be so weakened—that is to say, the impulses and inner forces had to be so weakened—that the original terrible impulse—ruled by Ahriman, that Ahriman's power (for originally it is Ahriman who gives rise to this wish) should be so far weakened that he could not express himself through man—*who would have thereby made himself permanently a servant of Shiva.* The sum total of these forces had to be so weakened that its expression in man only enables him to transpose himself into the being of another with his conceptions and ideas. When we try to force an idea of our own into the being of another, when we try to imbue another with a conception of our own, this conception impressed into the nature of the other is the blunted weapon of Cain which was thrust into Abel. And because this weapon was thus blunted it was made possible for that which was in an instant reversed into its opposite—*to pass over into evolution.* And thus by a slower evolution, through ever-increasing strengthening of his knowledge, man reaches at last the experience of something he was not permitted to express in the physical world because it there became a destructive impulse; stage-by-stage he develops first ordinary knowledge, then imaginative knowledge, which enters more into the being of another, then inspirational knowledge, which penetrates still more into the being of another—*until in intuitive knowledge he enters it entirely and lives on spiritually in the other being.*

"Thus, we gradually struggle up to the comprehension of what this Self really is. As to its innermost nature, the astral body is seen to be the great egotist; the Self is more than that—it not only lives for itself—*but wishes to pass over into others as well.* And knowledge, such as is acquired on Earth, is this dulled passion to enter into another, not merely to expand oneself and all that one is—*but to pass further beyond oneself into another.* It is egotism intensified and extended beyond itself.

"If you bear in mind what the origin of knowledge is, you will then understand that there is always the possibility of misusing it—*for if this is a true knowledge in the Self*—the moment it goes astray it is misused. Only by progressing, and making this penetration into another more and more spiritual, and the renunciation by the astral body which has expanded to world-interests, of this penetration into another's being, only by leaving his constitution quite untouched and placing his interests higher than our own, can we make ourselves ready for higher knowledge.

Moreover, we cannot recognize a being of the hierarchy of the angels, for instance, if we have not reached the stage when the inner-being of the angels interests us more than does our own. As long as we have more interest in our own being than in the being of the angels, we cannot recognize them. Thus we must first educate ourselves up to *World-Interests*, and then to interests that go even further, so that another can be more important and of more consequence than oneself. The moment we try to develop further in occult experiences, while yet remaining more precious to ourselves than the other beings we wish to know, that same moment we go astray. At this point, if you follow out this train-of-thought, you really come to a true conception of black magic; for black magic begins where occult activity is carried into the world without our first being in the position to expand our own interests into World-Interests—*without being able to value other interests more than our own.*

"Such things can really only be touched upon, so as to arouse conceptions concerning them; they are too important for more than this. I wished to show how we may gradually come to recognize in its true form, not in its Maya [illusion], that which dwells within us as astral body and self; for what a man experiences inwardly as his astral body is not the true astral body—*but merely the reflection of that in the etheric body.* And what a man calls his 'self' is not the True-Ego—*but a reflection of the Ego in his physical body.* A man only experiences reflections of his inner-being. If he were to experience the forms of his own inner astral body and Ego before he was sufficiently mature, impulses of destruction would be enkindled within him; he would become an aggressive being; the desire to injure would arise within him. And such things underlie all black magic. Although the paths followed by black magic are many, the effect they aim at is always something like a covenant with Ahriman or Shiva. We can only learn to recognize the astral body and Ego in their true form if at the same time we acknowledge the necessity of developing them and making them worthy of being what they ought to be. The innermost nature of the astral body is egotism; but it should become our ideal to be permitted to be an egotist because the interests of the world have become our own. It must be our ideal to be allowed to enter into another being because we do not intend to seek our own interests—*but we find the other being more important than ourselves.* Self-education must go so far that we feel this upper picture in all its occult-moral significance; that we so gradually transform this picture which is our 'self,' that we can no longer be warmed by our own emotions, impulses, desires and passions—*but that with living our life in the astral body we enter the frosty solitude; we then thereby open ourselves to the warmth, to the warm interest which streams forth from the other worlds, and wish to unite ourselves with the beneficent forces proceeding from this other being.* This is at the same time the starting-point for a gradual raising of our self to the Higher Hierarchies in their true form. We do not attain to the Beings of the higher Hierarchies if we are not in a position worthily to confront the Imagination and Inspiration which has been described, and to bear seeing its opposite picture; that is, the possibilities in the depths of human nature when it was cast down from the Spiritual into the physical world. If we refuse to look upon the twofold picture of Cain and Abel below—our own self, and the representative of our Higher-Self—the mediator between our self and the higher Hierarchies—*we cannot ascend.* But when we are able to cultivate within our self the feeling indicated here, we then experience our Self, and this provides the entrance to the Higher Orders of the Hierarchies."

Occult Science, **Rudolf Steiner, Chapter V,** *Cognition of the Higher Worlds—Initiation,* **1909, GA 13**

"If the student of the spirit ascends upon the path into the higher worlds of knowledge, he notices at a certain stage that the cohesion of the forces of his personality assumes a different form from the one in the physical-sensory world, where the ego ['I'] effects a uniform co-operation of the soul forces, of thinking, feeling, and willing. These three soul forces stand always in a certain relationship to each other in the conditions of ordinary human life. One sees, for example, a certain object in the outer world. It pleases or displeases the soul. That is to say, of necessity the visualizing of a thing will be followed by a feeling of pleasure or displeasure. One may, perhaps, desire the object or have the impulse to alter it in one way or another. That is, the power of desire and will associate with visualizing and feeling. That this co-ordination takes place is caused by the ego uniting visualizing (thinking), feeling, and willing and in this way bringing order into the forces of the personality. This healthy order would be interrupted if the ego were to prove powerless in this regard; if, for example, desire should elect to go a different way from feeling or thinking. A human being would not be in a healthy soul condition who might think that this or that is right, but who might want something of which he is convinced that it is not right. The case would be similar if someone did not want what pleases him; but rather what displeases him. The human being now notices that on the path to higher knowledge thinking, feeling, and willing do indeed separate and each assumes a certain independence. For example, a certain thought has no longer an inward urge toward a certain feeling and willing. The matter is as follows. In thinking something may be perceived correctly, but in order to have any feeling or to come to a resolution of the will, we need again an independent impulse from ourselves. During supersensible perception thinking, feeling, and willing do not remain three forces that radiate from the common ego-center of the personality—*but they become three independent entities, three personalities, as it were*—one must now make one's own ego all the stronger—for it is not merely a matter of its bringing three forces into order—*but of leading and directing three entities.* This separation, however, must only exist during supersensible perception. Here again it becomes clear how important it is that the exercises for higher training be accompanied by those that give certainty and firmness to the power of judgment, and to the life of feeling and willing. For the person who does not bring these qualities with him into the higher world will soon see how the ego proves weak and unable to act as an orderly guide for thinking, feeling, and willing. If this weakness were present—*the soul would be as though torn by three personalities in as many directions and its inner unity would cease.* If, however, the development of the student proceeds in the right way the described transformation of forces signifies true progress—*the ego remains master of the independent entities that now form its soul.*—In the further course of this evolution the development continues. Thinking that has become independent stimulates the emergence of a special fourth soul-spirit being that may be described as a direct influx of currents into man, similar to thoughts. The entire Cosmos then appears as a thought-structure confronting man as does the plant or animal world in the realm of the physical senses. Likewise, feeling and willing that have become independent stimulate two forces in the soul that act in it like independent beings. Still another seventh power and being appears that is similar to one's own ego itself.

"This entire experience is connected with yet another. Before his entrance into the supersensible world, man knew thinking, feeling, and willing only as inner-soul experiences. As soon as he enters the supersensible world he perceives objects that do not express the physical-sensory—*but the psycho-spiritual*. Behind the characteristics of the new world now perceived by him stand soul-spirit beings. These now stand before him as an outer world, just as in the physical realm stones, plants, and animals stood before his senses. The student of the spiritual can now perceive an important difference between the world of soul and spirit that reveals itself to him, and the world that he was accustomed to perceiving through his physical senses. A plant in the world of the senses remains just as it is, whatever the human soul may feel or think about it. With the images of the world of soul and spirit this is, at the outset—*not the case*. They alter according to what the human being feels or thinks. In this way he gives them form that depends upon his own nature. Let us imagine that a certain picture appears before man in the world of imagination. If, at first, he remains indifferent to it in his soul, it then shows itself in a certain form. At the moment, however, when pleasure or displeasure is felt in regard to the picture, it changes its form. The pictures therefore, in the first instance, express not only what they are, independent of man—*but they reflect what man is himself*. They are permeated through and through by his own nature. The latter spreads like a veil over the supersensible beings. Although real beings confront him, he does not see them; but instead, his own creation. Thus he may have something true before him and, nevertheless, see something false. Indeed, this is not only the case in regard to what man notices in himself as his own essential nature—*but everything that is in him affects this world*. He may have, for example, hidden inclinations that do not come into evidence in life because of his education and character; they affect the world of the soul and spirit, which takes on a peculiar coloring through the whole being of man, no matter whether he himself knows much about this being or not. In order to be able to advance further from this stage of development it is necessary that man learn to distinguish between himself and the outer spiritual world. It is necessary that he learn to eliminate all the effects of himself upon his soul-spirit environment. This cannot be done otherwise than by acquiring a knowledge of what he himself carries into the new world. It is therefore important that he first possess true, thoroughly developed self-knowledge, in order to be able to have a clear perception of the surrounding world of soul and spirit. Now, certain facts of human development demand that such self-knowledge must take place quite naturally at the time of the entrance into the higher world. Man develops his ego, his self-consciousness in the everyday physical-sensory world. This ego now acts as a center of attraction for everything belonging to man. All his inclinations, sympathies, antipathies, passions, and opinions group themselves, as it were, around his ego ['I'], and this ego is also the point of attraction for what may be designated as the karma of man. If this ego were to be seen unconcealed it would show that certain forms of destiny must still be encountered by it in this and in subsequent incarnations, according to the way it has lived in the preceding incarnations and has made this or that its own. Invested with all this, the ego must appear as the first image before the human soul when the latter ascends into the world of soul and spirit. This Doppelgänger (double or twin likeness) of man must, according to a law of the spiritual world, emerge prior to everything else as his first impression in that world. One may easily make the law underlying this fact understandable if one considers the following. In the life of the physical senses man only perceives himself in so far as he experiences himself inwardly in his thinking, feeling, and willing. This, however, is an inner perception; it does not present itself to the human being like stones, plants, and animals. Also, man learns to know himself only partially through inner-perception. He has something in himself that prevents his having more profound self-knowledge. This is an impulse to transform immediately a trait of character if he, as a result of self-knowledge, must admit to it and does not wish to deceive himself about himself.

"If he does not follow this impulse, if he simply turns his attention away from himself, remaining what he is, then he, naturally, also deprives himself of the possibility of self-knowledge about the point in question. If man, however, penetrates into himself and confronts himself without deception with this or that trait, then he will either be in the position to improve the trait, or he will be incapable of doing so under the present circumstances of his life. In the latter case, a feeling will creep over his soul that must be described as—*a feeling of shame*. This is indeed the reaction of healthy human nature: it feels through self-knowledge various kinds of shame. This feeling has even in ordinary life a quite definite effect. The normally thinking human being will take care that what fills him, throughout himself, with this feeling does not become evident outwardly in effects—*that it does not manifest in outer deeds*. Shame is thus a force that impels man to conceal something in his inner-being and not allow it to become outwardly perceptible. If we give this due consideration, we shall find it comprehensible that spiritual research ascribes much farther reaching effects to an inner-soul experience that is closely related to the feeling of shame. This research finds that there is, concealed in the depths of the soul, a sort of hidden shame of which the human being is not conscious in physical-sensory life. This concealed feeling, however, acts in a similar manner to the feeling of shame in everyday life; it prevents the innermost nature of the human being from appearing before him in a perceptible picture. If this feeling were not present, the human being would perceive before him what he is in truth; his thoughts, feelings, and will would not only be experienced inwardly—*but would be perceived outwardly just as stones, animals, and plants are perceived.* This feeling is thus the concealer of man from himself, and at the same time it is the concealer of the entire world of soul and spirit. Owing to the fact that his inner-nature is concealed from him, he is also not able to perceive that by means of which he should develop inner organs in order to cognize the world of soul and spirit; he is unable so to transform his nature that it may unfold spiritual organs of perception.—If, however, through correct training man strives to acquire these organs of perception, what he himself is appears to him as a first impression. He perceives his Doppelgänger, his double. This self-perception is not at all to be separated from the perception of the rest of the world of soul and spirit. For in everyday life of the physical-sensory world—*the feeling characterized above acts so as constantly to close the door of the world of soul and spirit to the human being.* Even the mere attempt to penetrate into this world causes the feeling of shame—which arises immediately, but of which we do not become conscious—to conceal the part of the world of soul and spirit that strives to appear. *The exercises herein open the door to this world.* It is a fact, however, that this concealed feeling acts like a great benefactor of man. For all that man acquires of power of judgment, feeling-life, and character without spiritual-scientific training does not enable him to bear without further preparation the perception of his own being in its true form. He would lose through this perception all self-esteem, self-confidence, and self-consciousness. That this may not happen, we must take the necessary precautions which we do undertake, alongside the exercises for higher knowledge, in the fostering of a healthy power of judgment, feeling-life, and character. Through this regular training man learns to know so much of Spiritual Science—as though without intention—and, moreover, so many means for the attainment of self-knowledge and self-observation become clear to him as are necessary in order to encounter his Doppelgänger bravely. The student then only sees in another form, as a picture of the imaginative world, what he has already learned in the physical world. If he has first comprehended the law of karma properly in the physical world through his intellect, he will not be especially shaken when he now sees the beginnings of his destiny engraved in the image of his Doppelgänger. If man has made himself acquainted through his power of judgment with the evolution of the Cosmos and mankind and knows how, at a certain point-of-time of this evolution, the forces of Lucifer have penetrated into the human soul, he will bear it without difficulty when he becomes aware that the luciferic beings with all their effects are contained within the image of his own nature.—We see from this how necessary it is that man does not demand entrance into the spiritual world before he has understood, through his ordinary power of judgment developed in the physical-sensory world, certain truths about the spiritual world. The knowledge given in this book prior to the discussion about "Cognition of the Higher Worlds" should have been acquired by the student of Spiritual Science by means of his ordinary power of thought in the regular course of development, before he has the desire himself to enter into supersensible worlds.

"In a training in which no attention is paid to the certainty and firmness of the power of judgment, of the life of feeling and character, it may happen that the student encounters the higher world before he possesses the necessary inner faculties. In that case the encounter with his Doppelgänger would depress him and lead to error. If, however, the encounter was entirely avoided— something that might indeed be possible—and nevertheless he was led into the supersensible world—*he would then be unable to recognize that world in its true shape.* For it would be quite impossible for him to distinguish between what he carries over as projections of himself into things and what they are in reality. This distinction is only possible if one perceives one's own being as an image in itself, and if, as a result of this distinction, everything that flows from one's own inner-nature becomes detached from the environment.—For man's life in the physical-sensory world, the Doppelgänger's effect is such that he becomes immediately invisible through this feeling of shame that occurs when the man approaches the world of soul and spirit. As a result of this, the entire the world of soul and spirit is also concealed. Like a 'guardian' the Doppelgänger stands there before that world—*in order to deny entrance to those who are not truly capable of entering.* He may therefore be called the 'Guardian of the Threshold that lies before the world of soul and spirit.'—Besides the described encounter with the Guardian at the entrance into the supersensible world, man also encounters him when passing through actual physical death; and therefore, in the ensuing course of life between death and a new birth the Guardian discloses himself by degrees in the evolution of soul and spirit. There, however, the encounter cannot depress the human being;

because he then has knowledge of worlds quite different from those he knows in the life between birth and death.

"If man were to enter the world of soul and spirit without encountering the 'Guardian of the Threshold,' he might fall prey to deception after deception—*as he would never be able to distinguish between what he himself has carried over into that world and what in reality belongs to it.* For a proper training must lead the student of Spiritual Science into the realm of truth only, not into the realm of illusion. This training will of itself be of such a nature that the encounter must of necessity take place sometime. For it is one of the precautionary measures, indispensable for the observation of supersensible worlds, against the possibility of falling prey to deception and illusion.—It belongs to the most indispensable measures that every student of Spiritual Science must take; that is to work carefully on himself in order not to become lost in fantasy, and succumb to possible deception and self-delusion. Where the advice for spiritual training is correctly followed, the sources that may bring deception are at the same time destroyed.

"Naturally, we cannot speak at length here of all the numerous details that have to be considered in regard to such precautionary measures, as the important points can only be indicated. For the deceptions that have to be considered here are derived from two sources. They originate in part from the coloring of reality through one's own soul nature. In the ordinary life within the physical-sensory world there is comparatively little danger from this source of deception; for here the outer-world continually impresses its own form sharply upon our observation, no matter how the observer wants to color it according to his own wishes and interests. As soon, however, as man enters the world of Imagination, its pictures are transformed through his wishes and interests, and he has before him, like a reality, what he himself has formed, or at least has helped in forming. This source of deception is removed by the student's having learned to recognize, through his encounter with the 'Guardian of the Threshold,' his own inner-nature, which he might otherwise carry into the world of soul and spirit. The preparation that the student of Spiritual Science undergoes before his entrance into the world of soul and spirit acts in such a way that he becomes accustomed to disregarding himself even when observing the physical-sensory world and to permitting the objects and processes to speak to him—*purely out of their own nature.* Therefore, if the student has thus prepared himself sufficiently, he can calmly await the encounter with the 'Guardian of the Threshold.' For this encounter will be the final test to determine whether he feels himself really in a position to disregard his own nature when he confronts the world of soul and spirit.

"Besides this source of delusion, there is still another. This comes into evidence when one misinterprets an impression made on oneself. A simple example of this sort of delusion in the physical sense-life is the delusion that arises when a man sits in a railway coach moving in a certain direction and believes the trees and other objects of perception are moving in the opposite direction, while actually it is he himself who is moving with the train. Although there are numerous cases where such delusions In the physical sense-world are more difficult to correct than the simple one quoted, still, it is easy to see that within this world one also finds the means of disposing of such delusions when, with sound judgment, one takes into consideration all that may possibly contribute to an adequate factual explanation. The matter is different, however, as soon as one penetrates into the realms of the supersensible. On the other hand, within the world of the senses facts are not altered as a result of human delusion; therefore it is possible, by means of unprejudiced observation, to rectify the delusion by means of the facts. While in the supersensible world this is not immediately possible. If one wants to observe a supersensible process and approaches it with false judgment, one carries this judgment over into the process and it becomes so interwoven with the fact that it is impossible to distinguish one's judgment from the fact. For the error is then not within the human being and the correct fact is outside him—*but the error itself is made a component of the outer fact.* It cannot, therefore, be rectified simply by an unbiased observation of the fact. We are here pointing to what may be a superabundant source of delusion and fantasy for those who approach the supersensible world without proper preparation.—The student of the spiritual, besides acquiring the ability to exclude the delusions that arise through the coloring of supersensible world-phenomena with his own nature, must also acquire the ability to make the second indicated source of delusion ineffective. He can exclude what comes from himself if he has first recognized the image of his own Doppelgänger. He will be able to exclude the second source of delusion if he acquires the ability to recognize, from the inner quality of a supersensible fact, whether it is reality or delusion. If the delusion were to appear exactly like the actual facts, then a distinction would not be possible. This, however, is not the case. Delusions of the supersensible world have qualities in themselves by which they are to be distinguished from realities, and it is important that the student of the spiritual know by which qualities he can recognize realities. Nothing is more self-evident than the fact that anyone ignorant of spiritual training may ask, 'How is it at all possible to protect myself against delusion, when its sources are so numerous?' And he may continue to ask, 'Is there any proof for the student of the spiritual against the fact that all his professed higher knowledge is not something based on mere delusion and autosuggestion?' Anyone who asks such questions does not realize that in true spiritual training, through the very manner of its occurrence, the sources of delusion are stopped up. In the first place, by preparing himself the true student of Spiritual Science will acquire sufficient knowledge about what may cause delusion and autosuggestion, and thus be in a position to protect himself from them. He has, in this regard, more opportunity than any other human being to make himself prudent and capable in judgment on the path-of-life. Everything that he experiences causes him to disregard indefinite premonitions and suggestions. For this training makes him as careful as possible.

"Besides this, all proper esoteric training leads first to concepts about great cosmic events, and thus to things that make necessary the exertion of sound judgment, which becomes, at the same time, more refined and acute. Only someone who might refuse to go into such distant realms and preferred to abide with 'revelations' of a world near-at-hand might lose the strengthening of that sound judgment that gives him certainty in distinguishing between delusion and reality. All of this, however, is not yet the most important. For that is accomplished through the exercises themselves that are used in a correct spiritual training. These must be so arranged that the student is always consciously aware of what takes place in the soul during inner-meditation. In order to bring about proper *Imagination*, a symbol is first formed. In this symbol are still contained mental images of outer perceptions. The human being is not alone responsible for the content of these mental images; for he does not make them himself. Thus he may delude himself in regard to its origin; he may interpret its origin incorrectly. But the student of Spiritual Science removes this content from his consciousness when he advances further to the exercises for developing *Inspiration*. For herein he contemplates his own soul activity only—*which has formed the symbol*. Nonetheless, here also error is still possible. For through education, learning, and through other means man has acquired the character of his soul activity. But he cannot know everything about its origin. The student of Spiritual Science now removes even his own soul activity from his consciousness. If now anything remains in his consciousness, nothing is attached to it that cannot be surveyed. Nothing can intermingle with it that is not to be judged in regard to its whole content.

"In *Intuition*, the student of Spiritual Science has thus a criterion enabling him to recognize how a clear reality of the world of soul and spirit is constituted. If he now applies the signs of soul and spirit-reality thus recognized to everything that comes under his observation, he is able to distinguish between illusion and reality. He may be certain that by employing this law he will remain protected from illusion in the supersensible world just as it cannot happen to him in the physical-sensory world to mistake an imaginary piece of hot iron for one that really burns. It is taken for granted that one only takes this attitude toward the knowledge one regards as one's own experiences in the supersensible worlds, and not toward what one receives as communications from other persons and that one comprehends with one's physical intellect and sound feeling for truth. The student of the spiritual will take pains to draw an exact line between what he has acquired in the one way and what he has acquired in the other. He will receive willingly, on the one hand, the communications about the higher worlds and seek to understand them by means of his capacity to judge. If, on the other hand, he states something as his own experience, as his own observation, he will have tested whether this has confronted him with precisely the qualities he has learned to perceive by means of unerring *Intuition*.

"After the student of the spiritual has encountered the 'Guardian of the Threshold', further experiences await him as he ascends into supersensible worlds. First, he will notice that an inner relationship exists between this Guardian of the Threshold and the soul-power that, in the above description, has resulted as the seventh principle; for it has shaped itself into an independent principle. Indeed, this seventh principle is in a certain regard nothing else but the Doppelgänger, the Guardian of the Threshold himself, and this principle sets the student of the spiritual a special task. He has to direct and lead with his newborn self what he is in his ordinary self, and which appears to him in an image. A sort of battle against the Doppelgänger will result. The latter will constantly strive for supremacy. To establish the right relationship with this Doppelgänger and not permit him to do anything that is not under the influence of the newborn ego strengthens and fortifies man's powers. In the higher world, self-knowledge is different, in a certain respect, from self-knowledge in the physical-sensory world. Whereas in the physical-sensory world self-knowledge appears only as an inner-experience. On the other hand, the newborn self presents itself at once—*as an outer-soul phenomenon*. For man beholds his newborn self as another being standing before him—*but yet he cannot perceive it completely*. For whatever stage he may have reached upon the way into the supersensible worlds—*there are always still higher stages*. And therefore, at these subsequent stages he will perceive ever more and more of his 'Higher-Self'. As this 'Higher-Self', can thus only partially reveal itself to the student of the spiritual at any of these stages. The temptation is extremely great which overtakes the human being when he first becomes aware of some aspect of his 'Higher-Self,' to observe this 'Higher-Self,' so to speak, from the standpoint he has gained in the physical-sensory world. This temptation is even good and it must appear, if development is to proceed in the right way. We must observe what appears in the Doppelgänger, the 'Guardian of the Threshold,' and place it before the 'Higher-Self' in order to note the contrast between what we are and what we are to become. Through this observation the 'Guardian of the Threshold' begins to take on quite a different form. He presents himself as an image of all the hindrances that the development of the Higher-Self must encounter. The student will perceive what a load he must drag in the form of his ordinary-self, and if he is not strong enough through his preparations to say, 'I will not remain stationary here, but unceasingly strive to reach my Higher-Self,' he will slacken his efforts and shrink back before what is in store for him. He has plunged into the world of soul and spirit—*but now gives up his efforts.* He becomes a prisoner of the form that, through the Guardian of the Threshold, now stands before the soul. What is important here is the fact that in this experience he does not have the feeling of being a prisoner. On the contrary, he believes he experiences something quite different. The form that the 'Guardian of the Threshold' calls forth can be of such a nature that it causes the impression in the soul of the observer of having before him, in the pictures that appear at this evolutionary stage, the entire compass of all imaginable worlds, of having attained the pinnacle of knowledge, with no need of striving further. Instead of feeling like a prisoner he may feel himself as the immeasurably rich possessor of all the world mysteries. The fact that one can have such an experience that depicts the very opposite of the actual facts will, however, not astonish a person who keeps in mind the fact that, when he experiences this, he stands already in the world of soul and spirit and that it is a peculiarity of this world that events may present themselves in reverse order. (This fact was pointed out earlier in this book when life after death was discussed.)

"The figure that one perceives at this stage of development shows the student of the spiritual something in addition to what appeared to him in the first instance as the 'Guardian of the Threshold.' In this Doppelgänger all the peculiarities were perceived that the ordinary self of man has in consequence of the influence of the forces of Lucifer. Now, however, in the course of human evolution another power has entered the human soul through the influence of Lucifer. This is the power that was designated in an earlier section of this book as the power of Ahriman. It is the power that prevents the human being during physical sense-existence from perceiving the soul-spirit beings of the outer world lying behind the veil of the sensory. The form the human soul has assumed under the influence of this power is shown in a picture by the shape that emerges in the experience described. The person who is adequately prepared for this experience will be able to interpret it correctly; very soon thereafter another form will appear that we may call the 'Greater Guardian of the Threshold' in contrast to the already described 'Lesser Guardian.' This Greater Guardian tells the student of the spiritual that he must not remain stationary at this stage but must energetically work on. He calls forth in the observer the consciousness that the world that is conquered becomes truth, and is not transformed into illusion—*but only if the work is continued in an adequate manner*. If, because of incorrect spiritual training, a person was to enter upon this experience unprepared, then, in the encounter with the 'Greater Guardian of the

Threshold'—*something would pour into his soul that only can be compared to the 'feeling of immeasurable horror,' of 'boundless fear.'*

"Just as the student of the spiritual [with the feeling of shame] in his encounter with the 'Lesser Guardian of the Threshold' is afforded the possibility of testing whether or not he is protected against delusions arising from the intermingling of his own being with the supersensible world, so can he also test himself by the experiences [with the feeling of fear] that finally lead to the 'Greater Guardian of the Threshold' whether he is capable of mastering the delusions described above as coming from the second source. If he is able to withstand the gigantic illusion that has been conjured up before him—*that the picture world he has gained is a rich possession, while in reality he is only a prisoner*—if he is able to resist this delusion, he is then, during the progressing course of his development, guarded from mistaking illusion for reality.

"The 'Guardian of the Threshold' will assume, to a certain degree, an individual shape for each human being. The encounter with him corresponds indeed to the experience by which the personal character of the supersensible observations is overcome and through which the possibility is given of entering a region of experience that is free from personal coloring and applies to every human being.

"If the student of the spiritual has had the above described experiences, he is capable of distinguishing, within the surrounding world of soul and spirit, between himself and what lies outside him. He will then recognize that it is necessary to comprehend the cosmic process described in this book, in order to understand man and his life. Indeed, we understand the physical body only when we recognize how it has been fashioned during the Saturn, Sun, Moon, and Earth evolutions.

We understand the etheric body when we follow its formations through the Sun, Moon, and Earth evolutions. Moreover, we understand what at present is connected with the Earth evolution when we know how everything has unfolded itself step-by-step. Through spiritual training the student is placed in the position to recognize the relationship of everything that exists in the human being to corresponding facts and beings of the world outside him. For it is a fact that every member of the human organism stands in a relationship to the whole world surrounding it. In this book it has only been possible to indicate the facts in a sketchy outline. We must, however, consider that the human physical body, for example, was present during the Saturn evolution only in its rudimentary beginnings. Its organs—the heart, the lungs, the brain—developed later out of these beginnings during the Sun, Moon, and Earth evolutions. The heart, lungs, and the other organs are thus related to the Sun, Moon, and Earth evolutions. It is quite the same with the members of the etheric and astral/soul body, the sentient soul, and the other principles. Man is fashioned from the entire surrounding world, and every part of him corresponds to a process or being of the outer world. At the corresponding stage of his development the student becomes acquainted with this relationship between his own being and the great world. We may designate this stage of cognition as the becoming aware of the correspondence between the 'lesser world,' the Microcosm, which is the human being himself, and the 'greater world,' the Macrocosm. If the student has struggled through to such a stage of knowledge, a new experience may occur for him. He begins to feel as though he were inter-grown with the entire cosmic structure, in spite of the fact that he feels himself in his complete independence. This feeling is a merging with the entire Cosmos, a becoming one with it, but without

losing one's own essential being. This stage of development may
be designated as the 'becoming one with the Macrocosm.' It
is significant that this becoming *one*, this union—*is not to be
thought of as though through it the individual consciousness were
to cease and the human being were to flow out into the Universe
and thereby merging with it.* Such a thought would be merely the
expression of an opinion springing from the untrained power of
judgment.—The stages of higher knowledge, in the sense of the
process of initiation that has been described in this book, may
now be enumerated as follows:

1. Study of Spiritual Science, in which one employs one's
   power of judgment gained in the physical-sensory world.
2. *Acquiring Imaginative knowledge. [Moral Imagination]*
3. *Reading the 'Occult Script'—corresponding to Inspiration.
   [Moral Inspiration]*
4. *Living into the spiritual environment—corresponding to
   Intuition. [Moral Intuition]*
5. *Knowledge of the relationships between Microcosm and
   Macrocosm.*
6. *Union with the Macrocosm. [Without the loss of
   individuality]*
7. *Total experience of all previous experiences as a
   fundamental mood of the soul.*

"These stages need not be thought of as successive
experiences. On the contrary, the training may proceed in such
a way that, in accordance with the individuality of the student
of the spiritual, he may have reached only a certain degree of
perfection in a preceding stage when he begins exercises that
correspond to a subsequent stage. It may well happen, for

example, that the student has only gained a few Imaginations with certainty, yet he already performs exercises leading to Inspiration, Intuition, or the cognition of the relationship between Microcosm and Macrocosm.

"If the student of the spiritual has experienced Intuition, he not only knows the images of the psycho-spiritual world, he cannot merely read their connections in the 'occult script'; *but he attains to knowledge of the spiritual beings themselves through whose co-operation the world, to which the human being belongs, comes into existence.* In this way he learns to know himself in the form he possesses as a spiritual being in the world of soul and spirit. He has struggled through to a perception of his Higher-Ego, and he has become aware of how he has to continue his efforts in order to control his Doppelgänger, the 'Guardian of the Threshold.' He has, however, also encountered the 'Greater Guardian of the Threshold,' who stands before him as an ever present exhorter to further effort. This 'Greater Guardian' becomes the ideal toward which he strives. If this feeling emerges in the student of the spiritual, he has then acquired the possibility of recognizing Whom it is that stands there before him as the 'Greater Guardian of the Threshold.' *To the perception of the student of the spiritual this Guardian now transforms himself into the form of the Christ,* whose Being and participation in Earth evolution has been made clear in the previous chapters of this book. The student is now initiated into the exalted mystery that is linked with the name of the Christ. The Christ shows Himself to the student as the 'great ideal of man on Earth.'—If thus through intuition the Christ is recognized in the spiritual world, what occurred historically on Earth in the Fourth Post-Atlantean evolutionary Period—the Greco-Latin Period—also becomes comprehensible. The way in which, at that time, the exalted Sun

Being, the Christ, has intervened in the Earth evolution and how he continues to work within this evolution becomes the personally experienced knowledge of the student of the spiritual. It is thus a revelation of the meaning and significance of Earth evolution that the student receives through Intuition. The way to knowledge of the supersensible worlds, which is described here, is one that every human being can follow, no matter what the situation in which he may find himself within the present-day conditions of life. When describing such a path we must consider that the goal of knowledge and truth is the same in all ages of Earth evolution; but that the starting points of man have been different in different ages. If the human being wishes to tread the path to the spiritual world he cannot at present begin at the same starting-point as, for example, the would-be initiate of ancient Egypt. Therefore, the exercises that were imposed upon the student of the spiritual of ancient Egypt cannot be carried out by the modern man without modification. For since that time, human souls have passed through various incarnations, and this advance from incarnation to incarnation is not without meaning and significance. Therefore the faculties and qualities of souls alter from incarnation to incarnation. Whoever considers human historical life, be it only superficially, is able to notice that since the twelfth and thirteenth centuries A.D. all life-conditions have changed when compared with previous centuries; that opinions, feelings, and also abilities of human beings have become different from what they were previously. The path to higher knowledge described here is eminently fit for souls who incarnate in the immediate present. It is one that places the point-of-departure for spiritual development just where the human being now stands in any situation presented by modern life.—Progressive evolution leads mankind in regard to the path to higher knowledge from period-to-period to ever changing forms, just as outer life changes its forms, and at all times a perfect harmony must prevail between outer life and initiation."

Secrets of the Threshold, **Rudolf Steiner, Lecture VIII, Munich, August 31, 1913, GA 147**

"Every impulse and tendency of human evolution changes from age to age; in the same way, as I have often pointed out, the ahrimanic and luciferic influences also change. Our epoch [5th Post-Atlantean Period, 1,414 A.D.-3,574 A.D.] is to some degree a sort of reversed repetition of the Egyptian-Chaldean age [3rd Post-Atlantean Period, 2,907 B.C.-747 B.C.]; but as a reversed repetition the luciferic and ahrimanic forces generally play a different role today in the external culture. During the ancient Egyptian-Chaldean age the human soul, looking out on what was happening, could say: From one side the ahrimanic influence is coming; from another, the luciferic. In this ancient civilization the distinction, outwardly, could still be made. However, by the Greco-Roman age [4th Post-Atlantean Period, 747 B.C.-1,414 A.D.] one can say that Lucifer and Ahriman confront the human soul directly and hold themselves in balance there. Anyone who enters deeply into the fundamental nature of the Greco-Roman civilization will be able to observe the state of balance between Lucifer and Ahriman. But in our time it has changed again. Lucifer and Ahriman now are in league together in a kind of partnership in the outer world. Before these forces reach the human soul, they are knotted together externally. In ancient times the spheres of influence from Ahriman and Lucifer were quite separate; but nowadays we have them tangled and knotted together within the development of our civilization. In light of this, it is extremely difficult for a human being to unravel this entanglement and find a way out of it. For everywhere in our current cultural milieu we find luciferic and ahrimanic threads interwoven in a chaotic mixture, stirring up a great deal of violent political agitation and even playing into many of the abstract ideas and superficial proceedings that are in full swing now and in times to come; and so, until we are clear about this, we will not be able to form a sound judgment of the conditions around us.

"In the times we are now living we need to be watchful of this chaotic entanglement of luciferic and ahrimanic threads. For no one today is more challenged to come to terms with these forces than he who is on the path of spiritual knowledge, he who is trying to arm his soul with clairvoyant capacities in order to discover something he cannot know with his ordinary consciousness—*the real being of man.* This must always be the true goal of Spiritual Science. From the descriptions already given, it is evident that as soon as a person approaches the higher worlds, he has to step across a threshold. As an Earth-being who has made his soul clairvoyant, he must go back and forth across that threshold and know how to conduct himself rightly in the spiritual world on the far side, as well as on this side in the physical world. Both in lectures and now repeatedly in our Mystery Dramas, this important threshold experience has been referred to as the meeting with the 'Guardian of the Threshold.'

"A person can actually ascend into the spiritual worlds—this has often been said—and have quite a few experiences there without having a meeting with the Guardian, something that is partly terrifying—but on the other hand highly significant—indeed of infinite importance for the sake of a clear, objective perception of those worlds. I have pointed to this and everything connected with it in my book, *The Threshold of the Spiritual*

World, at least as far as I could while treating the material in an aphoristic way. I have gone further in the course of these lectures, and now I should like to add only a few details to characterize the Guardian of the Threshold. Should I try to describe everything about the meeting with the Guardian, I would indeed have to hold another long cycle of lectures.

"May I point out again that when a human being leaves his physical body in which he lives with the physical world around him, he enters the elemental world and lives in his etheric body, just as in the physical world he lives in the physical body. Then when he leaves the etheric body clairvoyantly, he lives in the astral body surrounded by the spiritual world. We have pointed out that on leaving the astral body the human being can then be within his True-Ego [True-I]. Around him will be the supra-spiritual world. When he enters this world, he has finally attained what he has always possessed in the depths of his soul—*his True-Ego*. He reaches now the spiritual world in such a way that his True-Ego, his other-self, is revealed, actually enveloped in the element of living thought-being.

"All of us walking about on the physical plane have this other self within us; but our ordinary consciousness not only is not aware of it but cannot know that we will not perceive it until we ascend into the spiritual and supra-spiritual worlds. For our True-Ego is actually our constant companion within us; but when we meet it on the threshold of the spiritual world, it is there in a remarkable way, in fact one can say, decked out quite peculiarly. There on the threshold our True-Ego is able to clothe itself in all our weaknesses, all our failings, everything that induces us to cling with our whole being either to the physical sense world or at least to the elemental world. Thus, we confront our own True-Ego on the threshold.

"Abstract Theosophy can simply say: that is oneself, the other-self, the True-Ego. But in the face of the actual reality, we won't find much meaning in the phrase: *it is oneself.* Of course, we all move about in the spiritual world in the form of our other-self; but there we are entirely another. When we dwell consciously in the physical world, our other-self is actually very much another, a stranger to us, a being that is much more foreign to us than any other person on Earth. And this other-self, this True-Ego, decks itself out in our weaknesses, in everything we should really forsake but don't wish to forsake, habits of the physical sense existence that we still hang on to when we wish to cross the threshold. And there on the threshold we actually meet a spirit being different from all other spiritual beings we could meet in the supersensible worlds. The other beings appear to us in coverings more appropriate to their nature than those of the Guardian of the Threshold. He arrays himself in everything that arouses in us not only anxiety and distress but also disgust and loathing. He clothes himself in our weaknesses, in things that bring us to admit: Our fear of separating from him makes us shudder, or it makes us blush, overcome with shame, to have to look at what we are, at what the Guardian has wrapped himself in. While indeed this is a meeting with oneself, it is more truly the meeting with another entity.

"To get past the Guardian of the Threshold is not at all easy. Actually, it is much easier to behold the spiritual world than it is to behold it rightly and truthfully. To catch a few impressions of the spiritual world, especially in our modern time, is not all that difficult. To enter that world, however, in such a way that we behold it in its full reality, we must be well prepared for the meeting with the Guardian, however long it delays in coming to us—*for then we will experience the spiritual world correctly.*

Most people, or at least very many of them get as far as the Guardian. The important point is that we should come to him consciously. Every night we stand unconsciously before the Guardian. Certainly, he is a great benefactor of mankind in not allowing himself to be seen; for very few people could endure it. To bring into consciousness what we experience every night unconsciously—*is to meet the Guardian of the Threshold.* People usually get just to the edge of the boundary where, one can say, the Guardian stands. But at that moment, something very peculiar happens to the soul: it perceives this moment in a twilight state between consciousness and unconsciousness and will not allow it to come to full consciousness. On that borderline the soul has the impulse to see itself as it really is, clinging to the physical world with all its weaknesses and faults, but this is unbearable. Before the event can become fully conscious, the soul—through its utter loathing—deadens, as it were, its awareness. (Such moments of the soul's obliterating its consciousness are the best points of attack for the ahrimanic beings.)

"We come indeed to the Guardian of the Threshold by developing a sense-of-self that is especially strong and forceful. We have to strengthen our sense-of-self, if we wish to rise into the spiritual world. But in the process of strengthening our sense-of-self, we also strengthen all the tendencies, habits, weaknesses and prejudices that are held back and limited in the external world through our education, through custom and through the outward culture. On the threshold, the luciferic impulses assert themselves strongly from within, and when the human soul tends to deaden its awareness, Lucifer immediately unites with Ahriman, with the result that the entrance to the spiritual world is barred.

"If a person with a healthy inner-life searches out the insights of Spiritual Science without dwelling in a state of morbid craving for spiritual experiences, nothing particularly harmful will happen at the boundary line. If he attends to everything that should be attended to in the form of rightful, genuine Spiritual Science, nothing more will happen than that Lucifer and Ahriman will balance each other for the striving soul at the threshold and the soul simply will not enter the spiritual world. But when the person has a special craving to get in, a so-called 'nibbling at the spiritual world' can take place. Ahriman then, condensing what the soul has 'nibbled,' pushes into the soul's consciousness what otherwise couldn't enter it. With this, the person experiences in condensed form what he has taken from the spiritual world, so that it looks exactly like a reproduction of physical sense impressions. In short, he will be the victim of hallucinations and illusions; he will believe he has approached a spiritual world, because he has come as far as the Guardian of the Threshold. However, he has not passed the Guardian—*but has been thrown back because of his 'nibbling' at the spiritual world*. Everything he took in has condensed to what could contain genuine pictures of that world—*but does not contain the most important element*—the element that will guarantee the soul a clear perception of the truth and the value of what he sees.

"In order to pass the Guardian of the Threshold in the right way, it is absolutely necessary to develop self-knowledge: *truly genuine, unsparing self-knowledge*. It is a neglect of one's duty to the progress of evolution if one refuses to rise into the spiritual worlds, should karma make it possible in this present incarnation. It would indeed be wrong to say to oneself, 'I shall not enter the spiritual worlds for fear of going astray.' We should strive as intensely as we can to enter them. On the other hand, we must clearly understand that we may not shrink from what the human being is most apt and most willing to shrink back from: *genuine, truthful self-knowledge*. Nothing is actually so difficult in life as plain, honest self-knowledge...

"…As soon as a person comes into those worlds and finds himself in a region of loathsome things, it would then be best for him to face them boldly, with courage, while admitting to himself, 'Yes, I have indeed carried all this egoism up into the higher worlds, it would truly be best for me to face this egoism boldly and honestly.' But the human soul usually tends to shake off these repulsive things before becoming thoroughly conscious of them. We can say that developing truly genuine love and thoughtful, honest compassion are the right preparation for the soul that wants to find its way clairvoyantly into the spiritual worlds. When you reflect a little on how hard it is to acquire true compassion and the true capacity for love in this world of ours, you will not find these words completely unimportant.

"We should be clear that these descriptions, characterizing our crossing the threshold into the spiritual world, will lead to a truly genuine knowledge of the being of man. It is only through such descriptions that we will discover what man really is, and discover too our relationship to the way the human being approaches the higher, spiritual worlds, this time between death and a new birth, in a somewhat different but still natural way."

Lectures to the First Class, **Rudolf Steiner, Volume III, Lecture XXII, (Recapitulation of Lesson III), Dornach, September 11, 1918, GA 270**

"…Once the Guardian of the Threshold, at the edge of the abyss-of-being, has shown us how the forces of our inner humanity—willing, feeling, thinking—appear to the eyes of the Beings of the spiritual world; after the Guardian has shown us how in the present time's consciousness we have not awakened to our full humanity in respect to these forces if they are inwardly observed; but that these forces appear to the divine-spiritual powers as the three beasts, which are shown to us by the Guardian of the Threshold; after the Guardian of the Threshold has placed this shattering view before our souls, he shows us the path forward; which leads to ennoblement in self-knowledge, and which must be followed if the exhortation 'O man, know thyself' is to be realized.

"After he first showed us how we should stand in respect to our thinking, feeling and willing, he shows us—in the mantric verses which were cited at the end of the previous lesson in this Michael-School—how we are first to delve down into our thinking; but that this thinking is of an illusory nature [Scheineswesen] that cannot bear our True-Self; but how we are then interwoven out in the cosmic-ether and are at least able to revere those guiding beings who lead us from Earth-life to Earth-life.

"Then he shows us how we can delve down into feeling, how in feeling being and seeming are united, how there our being—selfhood in the good sense—arises with half its strength; how, however, we should understand that not only what is perishable and seeming in our being arises, but also the life-forces of the world, of the Cosmos.

"Only when we descend into the will do we feel being streaming into our selfhood. Seeming transforms itself into being. It descends into the will, and we feel the Cosmic-Creating-Powers streaming through our will…

"After the Guardian of the Threshold has presented this to our soul, he makes us aware of how we should integrate ourselves into the Cosmos, into the world with all its forces if we want to advance in spiritual knowledge. For what is within us is at first not distinguishable according to its place, whereas in the Cosmos it is ordered. In the Cosmos we can indicate the definite place. Within us everything is interwoven. But we do not achieve real knowledge if we do not rise up to the cosmic forces and the cosmic powers—if we remain subjective in ourselves, remaining in our own skin, if we do not go out of ourselves and let our body become the whole world. Then will our soul, our narrow humanity, feel itself to be a member of the Cosmos. The spirit will integrate our narrow humanity into the whole Cosmos, into the whole world.

"We must carry this out, as the Guardian of the Threshold indicates when he shows us how from the depths of the Earth, which draws all the beings by gravity, forces arise which also draw us down, which bind our will to the Earth if we don't make ourselves free by inner striving. Our gaze goes earthward if we want to localize our will. We must feel ourselves one with the Earth's gravity, feel drawn by the Earth and make the effort to free ourselves from the Earth's gravity if we want to let our will to be one with the Cosmos...

"And in wanting to integrate our feeling into the Cosmos, he does not direct us to the depths, but to the horizontal reaches of the world, where the forces swing from West to East, from East to West, permeating us. These are the same forces that grasp our feeling. We must feel the divine godly powers, who send their spiritual light in these pulsing waves from the horizontal directions if we wish to integrate our feeling into the cosmic distance. In order to integrate our willing into the vertical, feel it bound below and freed above, we must be able to send our feeling into the cosmic distance. *Then there will be light in our feeling.* Then something goes through our feeling which also goes through us, just as the Sun illuminates the Earth's air when it moves from East to West.

"However, in all that streams through us we must be loving. *The force of love alone, which lives and courses through humanity, can accomplish what is asked of us.* Then wisdom will course through us, and we will feel ourselves to be in the wide circles in which the Sun moves, as feeling humanity, as Self, strong for true, good spiritual creativity...

"And when the Guardian of the Threshold wants to speak to our thinking so that it integrates itself in the Cosmos, he doesn't direct us down to the will, which should rise upward; he doesn't direct us to feeling in the wide circle in which the sun moves— but he indicates the heights, the heavenly heights where alone the self ['I'] can live selflessly if it wants to receive the powers of thought in what comes with grace from above, if it wants to follow a higher striving. We stand below, the Word is above. We must be inwardly courageous to hear the Word; for only if we courageously strive for wisdom and knowledge does the Cosmic Word resound from above—*full of grace*—speaking about humanity's true wisdom."

The Lord of Karma— the Guardian of the Threshold

The self or 'I' is the focus of development and yet the self has many names, elements, and components: the "I Am," Ego, Lower-Self, Adam Kadmon Self, the Angelic Self, the doubles of the Lower-Self, the Higher-Self, Spirit-Self (Manas), the self of Life-Spirit (Buddhi), the Christened Self, the selfless self, and ultimately the highest self which is found in the Spirit-Human (Atman). All of these facets of the human self—from inception to fulfillment of spirit potential—are part of the biography of the "I Am." This includes both the 'absolute' cosmic "I Am" and the 'relative' earthly "I Am" found in every conscious human soul striving towards its Higher-Self. This biography of the 'self' is the greatest cosmological story ever told and each of us adds to this biography with every spiritual step we take.

What is the self, and what will the self become?" Only a panoramic view of the entire history of the Cosmic Christ could begin to answer these questions. The Pre-earthly Deeds of Christ would have to be addressed, as well as an explanation of the Nine Spiritual Hierarchies and their relationship to the Holy Trinity throughout the seven incarnations of the Earth. Also, we must come to understand the reality and significance of the Fallen angelic hosts within the sevenfold cosmic evolution.

At the center of this great sevenfold cosmic mystery is the spiritual scientific fact that Christ donated, through the combined forces and beings of the seven major Elohim (Exusiai, Spirits of Form), the form, function, and content of the human "I Am" for each individual human being. Then, through multiple sacrifices and great cosmic deeds, Christ sustained his creation by helping humans learn to *stand upright, speak, and think*. Through the Mystery of Golgotha, Christ birthed the "I Am" of humanity within human history. Since that time, Christ's Holy Spirit has accompanied each spiritual step that any human "I Am" has made back to the divine source from where Christ originally birthed the archetypal templates of our "I Am."

Christ the Son, like the Father God and the Holy Spirit, loves each individual personally *as a mother loves her child*. Each developing human "I Am" will one day advance and rise to through the realms of the angelic hosts. This is the goal of Christ's co-creation with the human "I Am." There is no way that these sacred realities can be dumbed down so that anyone, but an initiate, could understand the true impact of such profound wisdom.

The distinction between the Lesser Guardian and the Greater Guardian of the Threshold is often confusing. It would be hard to describe the distinction between the two without a historical reference point. Thus, we shall look at what an ancient Egyptian might have had as an experience when they crossed the threshold of sleep, initiation, and death.

The ancient Egyptian did not possess a highly developed "I Am" (ego) and therefore did not accumulate the karmic indebtedness that a modern Western soul often does. For when they crossed the threshold, there was not such a dramatic duality between the physical and spiritual worlds. The Lesser Guardian at that time was the Sphinx who could be seen at a distance by the common Egyptian as they crossed the threshold. The mystery of the Sphinx was the nature of the human being growing old and going from four legs to two legs, to three legs. Growing old, illness, and death were not feared by these ancient people like we fear them today. They still had natural clairvoyance and therefore knew that the spiritual world existed. For the ancient Egyptian death was simply a transition entering into a world they could still dreamily experience while awake. Therefore, death did not hold the fear, doubt, and hatred that modern humans bring to the threshold, and thus create the three terrible beasts dwelling at the threshold.

The ancient Egyptian barely went unconscious while crossing the threshold; whereas the modern person is terrified of death and self-knowledge and is often brain-washed to foster doubt, hopelessness, helplessness, homelessness, and fear that the future will overwhelm them. Thus, the modern person's consciousness is completely overwhelmed as they cross the threshold into sleep unconsciously. Just try to stay awake as you fall asleep, and you will eventually meet the Greater Guardian, which is usually quite terrifying at first; while one may encounter the Lesser Guardian upon waking from sleep. You are more cognizant of when you awake from sleep (the Lesser Guardian); and, on the other hand, the experience of falling into sleep is profoundly veiled (the Greater Guardian). In ancient times, just staying awake for three nights could bring on initiation and often dissolved the threshold before the initiate's consciousness.

When the ancient Egyptian died, they believed they would see the Jackal-headed god Anubis conduct the Weighing of Heart ceremony in the Hall of Maat; whereby he would weigh the heart (Ib) of the deceased on a 'scale' against the weight of an ostrich feather; symbolizing Maat (Ma'at), the goddess of truth, justice, morality and harmony. A heavy heart indicated that the person had used their "I Am" (ego) in selfish ways and thus accumulated karma (weight) that must be rectified. Thus, the soul was judged by Anubis and his fate in the spiritual world was declared by the weight of karma brought to Anubis by the dying soul. Anubis then determined whether the soul belonged to the Akhu, the 'blessed dead' who followed the code of Maat; and therefore deserved to enter the after-life and the Kingdom of Osiris. If, on the other hand, the heart was deemed unworthy by being heavier than the feather, it was to be devoured by the goddess Ammit, the "swallower of the dead," a frightful creature with the forequarters of a lion, the hindquarters of a hippopotamus and the head of a crocodile.

In ancient Egypt, the Lesser Guardian was seen as the Sphinx and the Greater Guardian was seen as jackal-headed Anubis weighing the heart in the Hall of Maat before the divine recorder, the ibis-headed Thoth, the consort of Maat. During Egyptian initiation, Thoth/Hermes the great priest, wore a Jackal's head during the ceremony which was a pre-vision for the aspirant of what will happen when they die and meet Anubis face to face. It should be noted that whether in sleep, initiation, or death, the Egyptian encountered somewhat different beings than we encounter today when crossing the threshold because their "I Am" ('I' or ego) was only beginning to develop and their doubles (negative thinking, feeling, willing) were still in the early stages of development.

For the ancient Greeks we see that the hell hound Cerberus guarded the gates to the underworld of Pluto with three terrifying heads that are related to the three Doubles that arise to hound the aspirant at the threshold. The ferryman Charon was the Greek's Greater Guardian of the Threshold who judged the dead by whether they had a coin in their mouth, which made them worthy enough to cross the river Styx and enter the underworld where their reward, or punishment, awaited them. Cerberus was like the Sphinx and Charon was like Anubis. There are two stages to entering the spiritual world, one through sleep and initiation and the other through death itself—*thus we have the Lesser and Greater Guardians.*

There are many gatekeepers, doormen, tilers, guard dogs, dragons, and guardians who make sure that the lower elements of the physical world do not enter the refined world of the spirit. Every culture has a unique description of the two beings you meet when you temporarily cross the threshold or when you permanently cross it through death. Many Christians imagine that St. Peter keeps the Keys to the Pearly Gates of Heaven, and only if he finds that you are worthy does he open the gates for you to enter Heaven. The Archangel Michael judged Lucifer and cast him to Earth and carries not only the sword that struck the stone from Lucifer's crown but also the scales of divine justice. Michael is often considered to be the being we meet when we go to sleep or become a soldier of God (Christian initiate). Michael, with his guardian sword, makes us review our day in our nightly prayers and weighs our good deeds against the bad on his 'scales of right and wrong'—*our Christian conscience*. Thus, we go to sleep forgiven or not, with a guilty conscience or not. If we are pure of heart, we can commune with the saints and angelic hosts in the spiritual world through dreams. If we have a guilty conscience, we go into deep unconsciousness to hide from the 'voice of conscience' which is trying to wake you up through self-knowledge. These few examples could be expanded upon a great deal because Christian churches have many images of the Lesser and Greater Guardian from the many ancient traditions the church subsumed into their art, architecture, and practices.

Rudolf Steiner gives wonderful descriptions of the Lesser and Greater Guardians in many of his works, especially in his book *Knowledge of Higher Worlds and Its Attainment*. We offer in this book many quotations, with references from Steiner concerning the Guardian so that you have the original words in order to place his indications within the proper context. Before Steiner, it was Lord Bulwer Lytton's occult novel *Zanoni* that was the most referenced work describing the Dweller on the Threshold. Later, H. P. Blavatsky and other Theosophists like Dr. Franz Hartmann, T. Subba Row, and many others tried to elaborate upon the nature of the Dweller because it is so intimately connected to spiritual initiation and development. Spiritual initiation is not possible without encountering and understanding the Dweller (Guardian) and his three helpers (doubles of thinking, feeling, willing). Thus, we have added to this book numerous selections concerning the Guardian and the Dweller in the second half. But what is most important in this study is to understand the deeper nature of the Greater Guardian.

In his descriptions of the Greater Guardian of the Threshold, who Steiner indicates is Christ in our current age, we have the entire development of humanity spelled out in the most beautiful terms.

Christ now mitigates karma and teaches His followers to understand the karmic consequences, even as a person is doing a deed. In the very moment of action, Christ illuminates what the karmic outcomes will be. Christ also stands next to the person who listens for Christ's wisdom concerning our own personal karma and what must be done to 'tame the dragon' of the Lower-Self. Christ's actions as the Greater Guardian sometimes look like a stern Judge to those whose hearts are found 'too heavy' to get into heaven. For Christ serves as the veritable 'midwife' who is 'birthing' the self-knowledge the aspirant will need to take the next step on the path of spiritual evolution. Who better than the highest being we can know within our Solar System—the second person of the Holy Trinity—*the Second Logos that is Christ,* to be the compassionate judge of those souls who go through the Threshold of Death. For the Divine Being Christ endured death as a man upon the Hill of Golgotha to redeem all humanity, and the Earth, from succumbing to the forces of entropy and certain death; which, according to Rudolf Steiner, because humanity had descended much too far into materiality—*would have resulted in the end of human evolution by around 333 A.D.* Therefore, Christ is the most appropriate being to 'mother' His own children into the spiritual world. For Christ's example of overcoming death is the true antidote to the fear of death, the doubt of spiritual existence, and the hatred of self and others. Christ is the perfect 'Higher-Self' that lifts all others within his warm and radiant tide of love.

These new tasks (or deeds) that Christ has taken on are in keeping with the Pre-Earthly Deeds of Christ, the Mystery of Golgotha, and the Second Coming of Christ in the etheric realm. Furthermore, Christ has given us cosmic-memory and the capacity to glean that which is eternal from the physical world and carry those memories and capacities from one human life to the next. Christ, as the new Lord of Karma, can mitigate karmic indebtedness and balance human karma even in natural disasters, man-made disasters, plagues, and wars—*because He has the complete power of the Holy Trinity and the*

Nine Spiritual Hierarchies behind His decisions. Christ is already to be found within the etherized blood rising from the heart that warms the head, and is currently waging a battle within the etheric realm around the Earth where the souls of humanity are at stake. Many souls when weighed by Christ, the Judge of humanity's karma, will be found too heavy due to the 'millstone' of materialism that is around their necks. For their souls did not reach up into their spirit nature during their earthly life, and thus are condemned to a dark, unconscious after-life through their ascent through the planetary spheres—*after reliving their addictions and lower desires in the sub-lunar realm of Kamaloka.* The Great Counselor can work miracles for sincere, pure-hearted aspirants who wish to emulate the King on the 'throne of their hearts'—*Christ Triumphant.*

Only Rudolf Steiner, through his powers of scientific clairvoyance, seemed to have fully understood the evolving nature of Christ Jesus. The Pre-Earthly Deeds of Christ are only explained in detail by Rudolf Steiner; and those indications, plus his interpretations of the *Gospels* and his own *Fifth Gospel—constitute the most complete cosmology of the Cosmic Christ that is to be found anywhere in human history.* It is this 'Biography of the Cosmic Christ,' or what Rudolf Steiner called the 'Sophia of Christ—the Wisdom of Christ' that is the heart of what the evolving human "I Am" is to become. As the only being from the upper-realms of the Spiritual World to experience physical human incarnation, Christ descended from the highest to the lowest and is now ascending back to Heaven taking his followers with him back into those realms of the spiritual worlds where He came from. In other words, every stage of being a human with an "I Am," even into our future angelic, archangelic, and archai natures, will be embodied by the Christ ahead of us and He will prepare these stages for our ascension alongside the Holy Spirit. Through His human incarnation, Christ perfected and transformed each of the bodily vehicles (physical, etheric, astral, etc.); and now these radiant, transformed vehicles exist within the etheric realm that He is fighting to maintain against the

forces of materialism, death, and the annihilation of the human "I Am."
In light of this, many saints were over-lighted by one or another of
these perfected vehicles of Christ that can multiply endlessly and help
in the battle to claim the etheric realm for Christ and His followers.
This battle of Christ (and the Archai Michael) against Ahriman and the
forces of death are the 'second most important event in human spiritual
development' according to Rudolf Steiner.

The Sophia (Wisdom) of Christ is the 'spiritual midwife' of the
Pure Virgin Soul of humanity that longs to wed the Lamb of God in
New Jerusalem where the Tree of Life springs anew. But the soul must
first be prepared, become enlightened to some degree, and consciously
begin on the path of initiation to meet and commune with higher
beings in the spiritual world. Christ is now the supreme Lord of Death,
the Lord of Karma, and the ultimate Judge of the human soul.

Between Sophia and Christ we have been given the wisdom
and love to conquer the three frightening 'beasts' of the threshold,
which are simply the unredeemed karma of past lives rising-up and
asking to be purified, forgiven, and transformed into a being who can
develop new supersensible organs of perception. Once the aspirant
becomes an initiate, the beasts that were met at the threshold of the
Lesser Guardian can now become good friends serving to remind us
of what we must work on in order to tame the animal nature within
our earthly bodies. But just like the methods to deal with the fierce
beasts that the Tibetans describe in the Bardo realm after death,
the antidote is to know that the beasts are *you*, and that only love
and commitment to the path of spiritual development 'for the sake
of all sentient beings' is the clear way through. Embrace the dark
doubles dwelling within your soul, within the Lower-Self, and use
them as a springboard to rise into the spiritual world with gratitude,
awe, and wonder by transforming your lower desires into the higher
desire for enlightenment to gain wisdom in order to help all sentient
beings—*just as Christ Jesus did as a perfect example of human "I Am"
development.*

The human "I Am" is a, so-to-speak, 3-D holographic shard of the cosmic whole and thus will evolve into what we see as the grandeur of the heavens, both in the day and the night. For the whole solar system is mirrored within the human body and all that we see in the wide reaches of the Cosmos is also found mirrored in the human body, soul, and spirit. And so, whether we are looking at the birth of the human "I Am" in ancient times through the hierarchical gifts that gave us our minerals, plants, and animals, or whether we are looking at the biography of the human "I Am" throughout history, Christ is there helping shape, evolve, and sustain the development of His children—His "I Am" creations that He pours tremendous love into every moment of every day. So, it seems logical that what Steiner's clairvoyant perception has indicated, that Christ in our day is the Greater Guardian of the Threshold and the Lord of Karma, is certainly true and can be experienced by any clairvoyant who looks into the etheric realm, that realm Steiner also calls the Land of Shambhala.

In the lectures entitled, *From Jesus to Christ*, by Rudolf Steiner (Lecture III, Karlsruhe, Lectures from October 5-14, 1911, GA 131) we hear Dr. Steiner say:

> "What is this event? It consists in the fact that a certain office in the Cosmos, connected with the evolution of humanity in the twentieth century, passes over in a heightened form to the Christ. Occult clairvoyant research tells us that in our epoch Christ becomes the Lord of Karma for human evolution. This event marks the beginning of something that we find intimated also in the *New Testament* in *Acts* 10:42, "He will come again to separate, or to bring about the crisis for, the living and the dead."

"To testify that He is the one ordained by God to be judge of the living and dead"; we can also read in *II Timothy* 4:1, "Christ Jesus, who is to judge the living and the dead."

According to occult research, this is not to be understood as though it were a single event for all time which will take place on the physical plane. It is connected with the entire future evolution of humanity. And whereas Christianity and Christian evolution were hitherto a kind of preparation, we now have the significant fact that Christ becomes the 'new Lord of Karma,' so that in the future it will rest with Him to decide what our karmic account is, as to how our 'credits and debits' in life are to be resolved.

Faith, Love, and Hope: The Third Revelation to Mankind, Rudolf Steiner, Nuremberg, December 2, 1911, GA 130

"In our time, however, a change is approaching, an important change which can be described in this way. Christ is becoming Lord of Karma for all those who, after death, have experienced what has just been discussed. *Christ is entering upon His Judgeship.* Let us look more closely into this fact. From the world-conception of Spiritual Science we all know that a karmic account is kept of our life; that there is a certain balancing of the deeds standing on the credit side of the account the sensible deeds, the fine deeds, those that are good—and, on the other side, the bad, ugly, lying deeds and thoughts.

"Now it is important, on the one hand, that in the further course of a man's earthly life he should himself adjust the balance of this karmic account. But this living out of the result of his good and splendid deeds, or those that are bad, can be done in many different ways. The particular adjustment in our future life is not always determined after the same pattern. Suppose someone has done a bad action; he must compensate for it by doing a good one. This good action, however, can be achieved in two ways, and it may require the same effort on the man's part to do good to a few people only as to benefit a considerable number. To ensure that in future, when we have found our way to Christ, our karmic account will be balanced—inserted in the cosmic order—in such a way that the settlement of it will benefit as many people as possible—that will be the concern of Him who in our time is becoming Lord of Karma—*it will be the concern of the Christ.*

"This taking over by Christ of the judging of a man's deeds is a result of His direct intervention in human destiny. This intervention is not in a physical body; but on behalf of those men on Earth who will increasingly acquire the capacity of perceiving Him. There will be people, for instance, who, while carrying out some deed, suddenly become aware—there will be more and more cases of this from now on, during the next 3,000 years—of an urge to refrain from what they are doing—*because of a remarkable vision.* They will perceive in a dreamlike way what appears to be an action of their own; yet they will not be able to remember having done it.

"Those who are not prepared for such a thing to happen in the course of their evolution will look upon it merely as imagination run wild or as a pathological condition of the soul. Those, however, who are sufficiently prepared through the new revelation coming in our time to mankind through Spiritual Science—*through, that is, this third revelation during the latest cycle of mankind*—will realize that all this points to the growing of new human faculties enabling men to see into the spiritual world. They will also realize that this picture appearing to their soul is a forewarning of the karmic deed that must be brought about—*either in this life on Earth or in a later one*—to compensate for what they have done.

"In short, people will gradually achieve, through their own efforts, the faculty for perceiving in a vision the karmic adjustment, the compensating deed, which must come about in future. From this fact it can be seen that in our time, too, we should say, as did John the Baptist by the Jordan:— '*Change your state of soul*' [Metanoia]; for the time is coming when new faculties will awake in men.

"But this form of karmic perception will arise in such a way that here and there the figure of the etheric Christ will be directly visible to some individual—*the actual Christ as He is living in the astral world*—not in a physical body, but as for the newly awakened faculties of men He will manifest on Earth; as counselor and protector of those who need advice, help or solace in the loneliness of their lives.

"The time is coming when human beings, when they feel depressed and miserable, for one or other reason, will increasingly find the help of their fellows less important and valuable. This is because the force of individuality, of individual life, will count for more-and-more; while the power of one man to work helpfully upon the soul of another, which held good in the past, will tend constantly to diminish. In its stead the Great Counselor will appear, in etheric form.

"Therefore, the best advice we can be given for the future is to make our souls strong and full of energy, so that with increased strength, the further we advance into the future, whether in this incarnation—and certainly this applies to the young people of today—or in the next, we may realize that newly-awakened faculties give us knowledge of the great Counselor Who is becoming at the same time the Judge of a Man's Karma; knowledge, that is—*of Christ in His new form*. For those people who have already prepared themselves here for the Christ-event of the 20th century, it will make no difference whether they are in the physical body, when this event becomes a widespread experience, or have passed through the gate of death. Those who have passed through will still have the right understanding of the Christ-event and the right connection with it; *but not those who have thoughtlessly passed by this third great forewarning to mankind given through Spiritual Science.* For the Christ-event must be prepared for here on Earth in the physical body. Those who go through the gate of death without giving even a glance into Spiritual Science during their present incarnation, will have to wait until their next before gaining a right understanding of the Christ-event. It is an actual fact that those who on the physical plane have never heard of the Christ-event—*are unable to come to an understanding of it between death and rebirth.* They, too, must wait until they can prepare for it on their return to the physical plane. When, therefore, their present incarnation ends at death, these men in their essential being remain unconcerned in face of the mighty event referred to—the taking over of the Judgeship by Christ and the possibility of His intervening, in an etheric body, directly from the astral world in the evolution of mankind, and His becoming visible in various places…

"Hence, we have indicated that the Christ, in contradistinction as it were to the suffering Christ on Golgotha, is appearing now as Christ Triumphant, Christ the Lord of Karma. This has been foreshadowed by those who have painted Him as the Christ of the Last Judgment. Whether painted or described in words, something is represented which at the appointed time will come to pass.

"In truth, this begins in the 20th century and will hold good until the end of the Earth. It is in our 20th century that this judgment, this ordering of Karma, begins, and we have seen how infinitely important it is for our age that this revelation should come to men in such a way that even concepts such as faith, love, hope, can be given their true valuation for the first time."

From Jesus to Christ, Rudolf Steiner, Lecture X, *The Esoteric Path to Christ,* Karlsruhe, October 14, 1911, GA 131

"The event now to come, which can be observed only in a supersensible world, has been characterized in the words: —'*Christ becomes for men the Lord of Karma.*' This means that in the future the ordering of karmic transactions will come about through Christ. Ever more-and-more will men of the future feel:—

> 'I am going through the gate of death with my karmic account. On one side stand my good, clever, and beautiful deeds, my clever, beautiful, good, and intelligent thoughts; on the other side stands everything evil, wicked, stupid, foolish, and loathsome. But He who in the future will have the office of Judge for the incarnations which will follow in human evolution, in order to bring order into this karmic account of men, is the Christ!'

"And truly we have to picture this in the following way: After we have gone through the gate of death, we shall be incarnated again in a later period. We shall then have to encounter events through which our karma can be balanced; for every man must reap what he has sown. Karma is a just law. But what the karmic law has to fulfill is not there only for individual men. Karma does not only balance the accounts of each Ego; but in every case the balancing must be arranged so as to be in the best possible accord with the concerns of the whole world. It must enable us to give all possible help to the advancement of mankind on Earth. For this we need enlightenment, not merely the knowledge that the karmic fulfillment of our deed must come about. The fulfillment can take a form which will be either less or more useful for the general progress of humanity. Hence, we must choose those thoughts, feelings or perceptions which will pay off our karma and at the same time serve the collective progress of mankind. In the future it will fall to Christ to bring the balance of our karma into line with the general Earth-karma and the general progress of humanity. And this happens principally in the time between death and a new birth. But it will also be prepared for in the Epoch of time we are now approaching, before whose door we stand, because men will more and more acquire the capacity for a special experience. Very few are capable of it now; but from the middle of this century onwards, through the next 1,000 years, more and more people will have the following experience...

"This transformation of the human soul will derive from the Event which begins in the twentieth century and may be called the second Christ-Event, so that those persons in whom higher faculties have awakened will look upon the Lord of Karma. Some of you may say that when the Christ-Event of the twentieth century takes place, many of those now living will be with those who have fallen asleep, will be in the time between death and a new birth. But whether a person is living in a physical body, or in the time between death and a new birth, if he has prepared himself for the Christ-Event—*he will experience it.* The vision of the Christ-Event does not depend on whether we are incarnated in a physical body; but the preparation for the Christ-Event does so depend. Just as it was necessary that the first Christ-Event should take place on the physical plane in order that the salvation of man could be accomplished, so must the preparation be made here in the physical world, the preparation to look with full understanding, with full illumination, upon the Christ-Event of the twentieth century. For a person who looks upon it unprepared, when his powers have been awakened, will not be able to understand it. The Lord of Karma will then appear to him as a fearful judgment. In order to have an illuminated understanding of this Event—*the individual must be prepared.* The spreading abroad of the anthroposophical world-conception has taken place in our time for this purpose, so that men can be prepared on the physical plane to perceive the Christ-Event either on the physical plane or on the higher planes. Those who are not sufficiently prepared on the physical plane, and then go unprepared through the life between death and a new birth, will have to wait until, in the next incarnation, they can be further prepared through Anthroposophy for the understanding of Christ. During the next 3,000 years the opportunity will be given to men of going through this preparation, and the purpose of all anthroposophical development will be to render men more and more capable of participating in that which is to come."

The Three Paths of the Soul to Christ, Rudolf Steiner, Lecture II, *The Path of Initiation*, Stockholm, April 17, 1912, GA 143

"We are living in the Fifth Post-Atlantean Period [1,414 A.D.-3,574 A.D.]. In our Fifth Post-Atlantean Period men will add the great teachings of *Karma* to the other teachings—they will learn to *understand* their karma. In our Fifth Post-Atlantean Period, human beings are experiencing the third act which follows consistently after the Osiris act and the act of the Mystery of Golgotha. They will learn to grasp the idea:—

> 'I am placed on Earth through birth; my destiny is on Earth;
> I experience joy and sorrow; I must understand that what I
> experience as joy and sorrow does not approach me in vain,
> that it is my Karma, and that it comes to me because it is my
> Karma, my great educator. I look upon that which was before

my birth, which placed me in this incarnation, because this, my destiny, is necessary for my further development. Who sent me hither? Who will continue to place me on this Earth, into my destiny, until I have discharged my Karma? I shall owe this to the Christ that men can ever more be called to suffer their destinies, until they have discharged their Karma on Earth.'

"Therefore Jesus of Nazareth, out of whom Christ spoke, could not say to men:— 'Try to escape as fast as possible out of the physical body.' But rather, He had to say to men:— 'I will place you into your destinies on this Earth so long as you have not discharged your Karma. For you must discharge your Karma.'

"Men will learn as we approach the future that they were united with Christ before birth, that they have received from him the grace of discharging their old Karma in their incarnations. Thus did the men of the Fourth Post-Atlantean Period look up to Jesus of Nazareth as the bearer of the Christ. Thus, will the men of our time learn that the Christ will reveal himself ever more supersensibly, and will govern more and more the threads of Karma within the affairs of Earth. They will learn to know that spiritual power as that destiny which the Greeks could not yet recognize, which will bring men to the point of discharging their Karma in the most fitting way in their successive incarnations. As to a Judge, as to a Lord of Karma, men will look up to the Christ in the succession of incarnations, when they experience their destiny. Thus, men will stand in such a relation to their destiny that they will be stimulated increasingly to deepen their souls, until they can say to themselves:—

'This destiny is not allotted to me through an impersonal power, this destiny is allotted to me through that with which I feel myself related in my inmost-being. In Karma itself I perceive what is related to my being. My Karma is dear to me because it makes me better and better.'

Thus, one learns to love Karma, and then this is the impulse to know the Christ. Men first learned to love their Karma through the Mystery of Golgotha. And this will continue further and further, and men will learn more and more that under Lucifer's influence alone the Earth would never have been able to reach its goal—*that the evolution of mankind would have had to become more and more corrupt without the Christ.*"

Awareness—Life—Form, **Rudolf Steiner, Part I,** *Spiritual-Scientific Cosmology, Planetary Evolution,* **VII, November 1, 1904, GA 89**

"We have been considering the influences of which the human being is subject on the physical plane. Evolution in globes tends towards the physical plane. The human being, who is now at the mineral level, had to go through the preceding stages to prepare for his existence on the physical plane. In every area or on every plane we have to look at the part which matters. At present we are looking at the actual human being. In the seven consecutive states of the first planet (Saturn) he was quite imperfect, a kind of mulberry, a progressively developing form. First planet: Conscious awareness going down into the abyss. Spirits were involved in human evolution which had already gone through evolutions of their own and become dhyanic, which the human being will only be by the end of the

343 stages [7x7x7=343]. These spirits had gained all kinds of powers and energies.

"Human beings *take* in the first half of a cycle; in the second half they give back what they have taken. In the first half of the one cycle, the mineral world was thus separated out, since it was a hindrance to human beings. They were then using for themselves all the energy which would otherwise have served to develop the mineral world further; later on they absorbed this world again. In the second half of the cycle, human beings thus redeem the mineral world, metamorphosing it. They then give to the mineral world the achievements of their own evolution, having first separated that world out. Absolutely everything in human evolution is subject to the metamorphosis of taking and giving. This determines our ethical attitudes to the highest degree. Anything we make our own may only be taken so that it may be given back again later on.

"The dhyanic spirits had gone through the taking stage at an earlier phase in their evolution. This makes them giving spirits on Earth. From the very beginning they were makers, guides and brought order. When the mulberry (Old Saturn) divided into many orbs, those dhyanic spirits had to develop many orbs from that one orb. At the second stage (Old Sun), they put the orbs in order according to measure, number and weight. At the third stage (Old Moon) they established the law of elective affinity, of sympathy and antipathy among the orbs. The Dhyani of the fourth stage (Earth) rule over birth and death and over karma. They are Lords of Karma, the Lipikas who are above all taking or receiving, beyond sympathy and antipathy. They intervene at the fourth level of awareness, which is the level of daytime conscious awareness. Again and again new makers would come in and intervene at the evolutionary stage which the human being had reached.

"Let us be clear in our minds about the nature of those makers. Spirits who are at the human stage receive and give in alternation. We can only give something which we have previously received. The human being thus alternates between being subject to 'perception,' as it is called, and activity. Perception is subject to the law of taking; activity to the law of giving. The law of the makers, however, is the law of revelation. Their activity is known as 'revelatory activity.' (Arranging the world according to measure, number and weight, sympathy and antipathy, separating good from bad, and so on.)

"There is a major difference between these spirits which reveal themselves and us human beings. Seen on its own, human evolution proceeded in such a way that initially the human being was down in the abyss (physically an orb), which was followed by order being established with measure, number and weight, and so on. Human beings also become more spiritual at every higher level of evolution. If we go from the outside to the inside in human evolution, we come to the higher faculties.

"We said that human beings are evolving towards the principle of brotherliness. Today, at the fourth level, Manas emerges and Budhi and Atman are potentially there. At a later level Budhi will emerge, and at an ever later one, Atman. When brotherliness will develop around them from outside as they develop from the inside to the outside, they will apply these principles from the outside to the same degree as they are evolving from the inside. When the human being has developed Manas, for instance, Budhi will begin to shine out as a potential development. In developing Budhi, human beings reorganize the whole astral body; the other pole of Kama (Budhi) then develops. The Kama which previously filled the human being inwardly will go to the outside and surround him as Budhi. This is an inversion, the reversal of the astral. All Kama is received by benevolent powers which are directed towards the outside. Then Atman will appear in Budhi. The same outward-directed transformation will then come for the ether body. The ether body is able to act into the outside world, not only morally and beneficially; but also magically. It then gains magical powers, vital energies. The influence of Atman and Budhi causes the human being to be poured out into the world, he spreads out to benefit the outside world. A lodge based on brotherhood that is more highly developed has the ability to work magic in the world and influence the Life-Ether.

"At the next stage, Atman, the 'Divine Self,' will shine out. The human being will then be aware that he belongs not only to the Earth but to the whole Cosmos. He will develop *Logos Awareness*. He will be a world creator, with the ability awakening in him to control the physical world just as he was controlling the vital energy before. Initially the human being developed from outside in; then from inside out. When he will have come so far that he will be able to control his outer surroundings, he will be a dhyanic spirit. Initially powerless where his influence was concerned—*he will then be all-controlling ...*"

Foundations of Esotericism, Rudolf Steiner, Lecture II, September 27, 1905, Berlin GA 93a

"Before the human being as pupil is led to that point at which of his own choice he can work on his etheric body, he must at least, to a certain extent be able to evaluate karma in order to achieve self-knowledge. Meditation therefore should not be undertaken without continual self-knowledge and self-observation. By this means, at the right moment man will behold the Guardian of the Threshold: the karma which he has still to pay back. When one reaches this stage under normal conditions it merely signifies the recognition of his still existing karma. If I begin to work into my etheric body, I must make it my aim to balance my still remaining karma. It can happen that the Guardian of the Threshold appears in an abnormal way. This happens when a person is so strongly attracted to one particular life between birth and death, that because of the very slight degree of inner-activity he cannot remain long enough in Devachan. If someone has accustomed himself to be too outward looking—*he has nothing to see within*. He then soon comes back into physical life. His desires remain present, the short Devachan is soon over, and when he returns, the collective form of his earlier desires still exists in Kamaloka; he comes up against this also. He incarnates. The old is then mingled with his new astral body. This is his previous karma, the Guardian of the Threshold. He then has his earlier karma continually before him. This is a specific form of the Double. [Doppelgänger]

"Many of the popes of the notorious papal age, as for example Alexander VI, have had such a Double in their next incarnation. There are people, and at present this is not infrequent, who have their previous lower nature continually beside them. That is a special kind of insanity. It will become ever stronger and more threatening because materialistic life becomes ever more widespread. Many people who now yield themselves up completely to materialistic life will in their next incarnation have the abnormal form of the Guardian of the Threshold at their side. If now the influence of spirituality were not to be very strongly exercised, a kind of epidemic seeing of the Guardian of the Threshold would arise as the result of the materialistic civilization. Of this the neurotic tendency of our century is the precursor. It is a kind of losing oneself in the periphery. All the neurotics of today will be harassed by the Guardian of the

Threshold in their next incarnation. They will be pursued by the difficulties of a too early incarnation, a sort of cosmic premature birth. What we have to strive for in Theosophy is a sufficiently long time in Devachan, in order to avoid too early incarnations.

"From this aspect we must consider the entrance of Christ into world history. Previously, anyone who wished to achieve a life in Christ had to enter into a Mystery school. There a state of lethargy was induced in the physical body and only through the purified priesthood could there be added to the astral body what was still needed for its purification. *This constituted initiation.*

"But through the coming of Christ into the world, it came about that a man who felt himself drawn to Christ could receive from him something which could take the place of this old form of initiation. It is always possible that someone through union with Christ can preserve his astral body in so purified a condition that he is able to work into his etheric body without doing harm to the world. When one bears this in mind the expression 'vicarious atonement through death' receives a quite other significance. This is what is meant by the atoning death of Christ. Before this—*death in the Mysteries had to be suffered by everyone who wished to obtain purification.*[1] Now the One suffered for all, so that through the world-historic initiation a substitute has been created for the old form of initiation."

Note:

1. "...*death in the Mysteries had to be suffered by everyone who wished to obtain purification.*" This refers to the rites in the ancient Mysteries where the hierophants would bring the individual into a trance condition whereby the separation of the vehicles was directed by the hierophants; this in-turn would allow the individual to have the experience of the after-death state. This is also the spiritual-scientific basis of the Baptism rite that was conducted by John the Baptist.

The Four Mystery Plays, **Rudolf Steiner,** *The Guardian of the Threshold,* Scene 7, GA 14

The Guardian speaks:
"What unchecked wish doth sound within mine ear?
So storm men's souls when first approaching me
E'er they have fully gained tranquility.
It is desire that really leads such men
And not creative power which dares to speak;
Since it in silence could itself create.
The souls which thus comport themselves when here
I needs must relegate again to Earth,
For in the Spirit-realm they can but sow
Confusion, and do but disturb the deeds
Which cosmic powers have wisely foreordained.
Such men can also injure their own selves
Who form destructive passions in their hearts
Which are mistaken for creative powers,
Since they must take delusion for the truth
When earthly darkness no more shelters them.

(Thomasius and Maria appear.)
Thomasius:
"Thou dost not see upon thy threshold now
The soul of him who was the pupil once
Of Benedictus, and came oft to thee,—
Thomasius, although upon the Earth
It had to call Thomasius' form its own.
He came to thee, with thirst for knowledge filled
And could not bear to have thee near to him.
He hid in his own personality
When he felt near thee, and thus oft did see

Worlds which, he thought, made clear the origin
Of all existence and the goal of life.
He found the happiness of knowledge there
And also powers which to the artist gave
That which directed both his hand and heart
Toward creation's source, so that he felt
There truly lived within him cosmic powers,
Which held him steady to his artist's work.
He did not know that nought before him stood
In all that he created through his thought
Except the living content of his soul.
Like spiders, spinning webs around themselves
So did he work, and thought himself the world.
He once believed Maria in true spirit
Stood face to face with him, and yet 'twas but
The picture she had graven on his soul
Which like a spirit did reveal itself.
And when he was allowed a moment's glimpse
Of his own being, as it really was,
He gladly would have fled away from self;
He thought himself a spirit but he found
He was a creature but of flesh and blood.
He learned to know the power of this same blood;
'Twas there in truth, the rest was but a shade.
Blood was his teacher true; and this alone
Gave him clear vision, and revealed to him
Who was his sire and who his sister dear
In long forgotten ages on the Earth.
To blood-relations his blood guided him.
Then did he see how strongly souls of men
Must be deceived when they in vanity

Would rise to spirit from the life of sense.
Such effort truly binds the soul more firm
To sense-existence than a daily life,
Dull human dream existence following.
And when Thomasius could view all this
Before his soul as being his own state
He gave himself with vigor to that power
Which could not lie to him although as yet
'Twas but revealed in picture, for he knew
That Lucifer himself is really there
E'en if he can but show his pictured form.
The gods desire to draw near to mankind
Through truth alone; but Lucifer—to him
It matters not if men see false or true,
He ever will remain the same himself.
And therefore I acknowledge that I feel
I have attained reality when I
Believe that I must search and find the soul
Which in his own realm he did bind to mine.

(To the Guardian):
"So armed with all the strength which he bestows
I mean to pass thee and to penetrate
To Theodora whom I know to be
Within the realm that o'er this threshold lies.

The Guardian Speaks:
"Thomasius, think well what thou dost know.
What o'er this threshold lives is all unknown;
Yet dost thou know quite well all I must ask,
Before thou canst set foot within this realm.

Thou must first part with many of those powers
Which thou hast won when in thine earthly frame.
Out of them all thou canst alone retain
That which by efforts, pure and spiritual,
Thou didst achieve, and which thou hast kept pure.
But this thou hast thyself cast off from thee
And given as his own to Ahriman.
What still is thine hath been by Lucifer
Destroyed for use within the spirit-world.
This too upon the threshold I must take
If thou wouldst really pass this portal by.
So naught remains to thee; a lifeless life
Must be thy lot within the spirit-realms."

Secrets of the Threshold, **Rudolf Steiner, Lecture VI, Munich,
August 29, 1913, GA 147**

"We have seen how necessary it is—in order to cross the
threshold rightly and enter the spiritual world with clairvoyant
consciousness—to leave behind us all the perceptions of the
physical world as well as everything we ordinarily think, feel,
and will in this world. We have to be prepared to confront
beings and happenings whose characteristics bear no relation
at all to what can be perceived in the sense world. First, we
have to strengthen the soul and its faculties, and then these
strengthened, fortified soul faculties must be carried upwards
with us. When we cross the threshold into the spirit realm,
we must take something with us. We have pointed out that
everything the sense world can give us, as well as the ideas and
feelings we acquire there, are all images of what is perceptible to
the senses. Nothing we acquire in this way can be of use in the
spiritual world...

"We must therefore acquire concepts, feelings, and ideas for the realm of the spirit if we really wish to cross the threshold, and while these must indeed be invoked by the physical, they will nevertheless have to rise above the physical-sense realm. Then with strengthened soul we will cross the threshold and become familiar with this world already characterized as a place of living thought-beings, engaged in spiritual conversation. With our strengthened soul we will become familiar with a world of beings that consists of thought-substance; through this thought-substance they are more alive, more individual, more real than any human being on Earth. These beings within their thought-substance are just as real as any man of flesh and blood on the physical plane. We can gradually find our way in this world where a thought-language passes between one being and another, and where our soul is forced to carry on thought-conversations with the thought-beings if we want to arrive at a relationship with them...

"...But here it can be said: a person lives in his physical body in the physical world around him. When he comes away from it and has experiences outside the physical body, he is having those experiences in his etheric body with the elemental world around him; and when he comes out of that world as well, he is experiencing the spiritual realm in his astral body. With this experience—feeling oneself in the astral body—there will be a meeting in the spiritual world, the meeting with the other-self, the second self, of which Johannes Thomasius speaks at the end of *The Guardian of the Threshold,* and which stands throughout the whole action of *The Souls' Awakening* at the side of the first-self of Johannes Thomasius, summoning forth his experiences. Let me describe the essence of this other-self; it is what a person comes to recognize when he learns within his astral body to perceive

Esoteric Lessons for the First Class of the Free School for Spiritual Science at the Goetheanum, **Volume One, Rudolf Steiner, Nine Lessons given at Dornach, Switzerland February 15— April 22, 1924, Translated by Frank Thomas Smith, Anthroposophical Publications, 2021, GA 270**

"Behold! I am the only gate to knowledge.

"Oh Man, know thyself! Thus sounds the Cosmic Word,
Solemn in thy soul thou hearest it
Mighty in Spirit thou feelest it,
Who speaks so powerfully through the world?
Who speaks so tenderly within they heart?
Works it through the far-spread rays of space
Into thy senses' experience?
Sounds it through the weaving waves of time
Into thy life's evolving stream?
Is it thou, Oh Man, who to thyself –
Sensing in space, experiencing in time
This Word dost beget,
Feeling thyself a stranger
In the vast soul-void of space
Because the force of thought is ebbing from thee
In the destruction stream of time?

"Know first the earnest Guardian!
He stands before the gate of Spirit-Land,
Denying entry to thy senses' power
And to thy might of intellect,
Because in all thy senses' life

And in thy weaving of thoughts,
From the spirit-emptiness of space,
From time's delusive powers,
Thou first must find
With conquering strength
True being of thy being.

"I entered in this world of sense
Bringing with me the heritage of thought
The power of a god hath led me here

"From the Divine springeth mankind (ex deo nascimur)
I esteem the Father

"Death stands at the end of the way
"I will to feel the Being of Christ
He in the death of matter wakens birth of spirit

"In Christ death becomes life (in Christo morimur)
I love the Son

"Thus, in the spirit shall I find the Word
And in the world-becoming know thyself
Through the Spirit we come to life again (per spiritum sanctum
reviviscimus)
I unite with the Spirit"

(Freely-rendered translation by DJG)

knowledge. But then he used words which at first are dismaying for the soul.

"The Guardian calls us to stand close to him. He looks at us with earnest countenance. And he shows us how our willing, our feeling, our thinking appear before the countenance of the gods as imaginations. There this willing, this feeling, this thinking is not yet human; it is still animal-like. *There the self-knowledge is dismaying, even shattering.*

"But we must pass through knowledge of that self, which is the result of the errors embedded in us by our times, our cosmic time, in order to press forward to true self-knowledge.

"This erroneous self-knowledge, the knowledge of the self which we carry within us from the spirit of our times, is shown to us by the Guardian by letting the first of the beasts, which represents willing, to arise from the yawning abyss-of-being. Then, raising his hand and pointing to the yawning abyss-of-being, he lets the second beast arise, representing feeling. Again pointing to the yawning abyss-of-being, he lets the third beast emerge, which represents thinking.

"They arise one after the other thus:—

"The first beast—the true spiritual form of our willing, created by the fear of knowledge, which can only be overcome by having the courage for spiritual knowledge.

"And then the second beast—born from the hate of spiritual knowledge, which at the present time is in the subconscious of the Gemüt [soul, heart or mind] of all people, which can only be overcome by the right enthusiasm for knowledge, for the right heartfelt blaze of knowledge; whereas today nonchalance and tepidity in respect of knowledge, yes, hate of knowledge due to nonchalance and tepidity is in the hearts.

"And then the third beast—created in its ghostly nature by doubt about the spiritual world that today gnaws at the souls' roots, and which can only be overcome if knowledge awakens in itself the strength to create in one's own soul [Gemüt] the things of the spiritual world beyond…

"As long as we consider thinking as something living, we are not experiencing the truth; only when we consider our body as the coffin of dead-thinking, and we feel it deeply, are we experiencing the truth. This is what the Guardian of the Threshold at the yawning abyss-of-being tells us, whose words we will then hear, words which can serve us as a mantric verse. He says it to us with special intimacy.

"And when we turn from thinking and observe our feeling, then we must see and feel how normal feeling, which we believe is alive in us between birth and death, is only half alive, how it continually consumes and kills something in us, how in fact it makes us spiritually hollow. Thinking is dead, and feeling is half alive, it is basically only an image-form in us. And only when we feel that this earthly feeling is a weak, half-living reflection of the solar power that emits cosmic feeling throughout the entire Cosmos as general universal love, then only do we feel correctly about feeling. This the Guardian of the Threshold tells us privately, in intimacy.

"And only when we feel that our will, although it lives in us, is continually tempted and attacked by spiritual opposing powers, so that its strength does not serve the divine above, but the physical below; only when we feel these opposing powers, who wish to divert us in our will from our actual divine task and completely enmesh us in earthly existence, then we will feel how these opposing powers, by usurping our will, want to bring the future of the Earth under their power. If they were able to do it, if we were not alert enough to dedicate our will to the Divine, and not to the Ahrimanic earthly powers, then the Earth would become problematic for the gods to whom it has belonged from the its very beginning."

Lectures to the First Class, Rudolf Steiner, Part I, Lecture III, Dornach, February 29, 1924, GA 270

"It is quite different in the spiritual world. *You must first grow into the spiritual world.* For the spiritual world you must acquire the correct feeling of your own true reality. Then you will gradually be able to differentiate between truth and error, between reality and semblance of reality.

"When you sit down on a chair—at the moment you don't fall on the floor, but are able to sit safely on the chair, you know that in the physical world the chair is a real chair and not merely an imagined chair. The chair itself provides proof of its reality.

"That is not the case in the spiritual world. For why is it so in the physical world? Because in the physical world your thinking, your feeling, your willing are held together by the physical body. You are a threefold human being: *a thinking, feeling and a willing human being*. But they are all unified within each other by the physical body.

"At the moment when the human being enters the spiritual world, he immediately becomes a triple being. His thinking goes its own way, his feeling goes its own way, his willing goes its own way. So you can think in the spiritual world, have thoughts which have nothing to do with your willing; but these thoughts are illusions. You can have feelings which have nothing to do with your willing; but these feelings contribute to your undoing, not to your advancement.

"That is the essential thing, that when a person approaches the threshold of the spiritual world it seems to him that his thinking flies out into distant space and that his feeling goes beyond his memory.

"Consider for a moment what I just said. You see, memory is really something which comes very close to the threshold of the spiritual world. Let's say you experienced something ten years ago. It returns in memory. The experience is there again. You are justifiably satisfied, as far as the physical world is concerned, if you have a vivid memory of it. For someone who has entered the spiritual world, however, it is as though he pushes through the memory, as though he goes farther than the memory reaches. In any case he goes farther back than his memory of physical earthly life can reach. *He goes back beyond birth.*

"And when one enters the spiritual world, he immediately senses that his feeling does not stay with him. Thinking at least goes out into the presently existing Universe. It disperses, as it were, in cosmic space. Feeling goes out of the Universe and if one wants to follow feeling one must ask: Where are you now? When you have become 50 years old, then you have gone back in time farther than 50 years; you have gone back 70 years, 100 years, 150 years. *Feeling leads you completely out of the time in which you have lived since childhood.*

"And willing, if you take it seriously, leads you ever farther back in time, back to your previous Earth lives. That is something which happens immediately, dear friends, when you really come to the threshold of the spiritual world. The physical body ceases holding you together. One no longer feels within the confines of the skin; one feels split into parts.

"You feel as though your thoughts, which were previously confined by feelings, are streaming out into cosmic space and becoming cosmic thoughts. Your feelings seem to go back in time in the spiritual world between your last death and your present

Earth-life. And with your volition you feel yourself in your previous Earth-life.

"It is just this splitting of the human being—I described it in my book *How to Attain Knowledge of the Higher Worlds*—which causes difficulties upon entering the spiritual world, because your thoughts expand. They had previously been held together and now stream out into cosmos space. At the same time they become almost imperceptible. So one must achieve the ability to perceive the thoughts which have thus expanded.

"Feeling is no longer permeated by thoughts; for the thoughts have gone, so to speak. So your feeling can only turn prayerfully, with reverence and devotion, to the beings with whom you pass your life between death and a new birth on Earth. This is possible if one has cultivated such reverence for the spiritual world in life.

"But the moment one's volition, which wants to proceed to previous Earth-lives, takes over, the person meets a great difficulty in that he feels an enormous attraction for the contents of his lower nature. And here works most strongly what I previously said about the difficulty in being able to differentiate between semblance and reality. For the person acquires a strong preference for semblance. I'll describe it as follows.

"When a person begins to meditate, when he or she is really dedicated to the meditation, he would like to continue in tranquility. He does not want it to deprive him of life's comforts. Well, this desire not to be deprived of life's comforts is a strong producer of illusions and semblances. Because when you dedicate yourself completely to meditation, necessarily from the depths of your soul the question arises about your capacity for evil. One cannot do otherwise than to feel through meditation, through that penetration into the depths, everything you are capable of perpetrating. But the urge to deny this is so strong that one submits to the illusion that one is essentially a very good person."

Lectures to the First Class, **Volume III, Lecture XXII, (Recapitulation of Lesson III), Dornach, September 11, 1924, GA 270**

"After the Guardian of the Threshold has presented this to our souls, he makes us aware of how we should integrate ourselves into the Cosmos, into the world with all its forces if we want to advance in spiritual knowledge. For what is within us is at first not distinguishable according to its place—*whereas in the Cosmos it is ordered.* In the Cosmos, we can indicate the definite place. Within us everything is interwoven. *But we do not achieve real knowledge if we do not rise up to the cosmic forces and the cosmic powers*—if we remain subjective in ourselves, remaining in our own skin, if we do not go out of ourselves and let our body become the whole world. Then will our soul, our narrow humanity, feel itself to be a member of the Cosmos. *The spirit will integrate our narrow humanity into the whole Cosmos, into the whole world.*

"We must carry this out, as the Guardian of the Threshold indicates when he shows us how from the depths of the Earth, which draws all the beings by gravity, forces arise which also draw us down, which bind our will to the Earth if we don't make ourselves free by inner striving. Our gaze goes earthward if we want to localize our will. We must feel ourselves one with the Earth's gravity, feel drawn by the Earth and make the effort to free ourselves from the Earth's gravity if we want to let our will to be one with the Cosmos...

"And in wanting to integrate our feeling into the Cosmos, he [the Guardian] does not direct us to the depths—*but to the horizontal reaches of the world, where the forces swing from West to East, from East to West, permeating us.* These are the same forces that grasp our feeling. We must feel the divine godly powers, who send their spiritual light in these pulsing waves from the horizontal directions if we wish to integrate our feeling into the cosmic distance. In order to integrate our willing into the vertical, feel it bound below and freed above, we must be able to send our feeling into the cosmic distance. *Then there will be light in our feeling.* Then something goes through our feeling which also goes through us, just as the Sun illuminates the Earth's air when it moves from East to West.

"However, in all that streams through us we must be loving. The force of love alone, which lives and courses through humanity, can accomplish what is asked of us. Then wisdom will course through us, and we will feel ourselves to be in the wide circles in which the Sun moves, as feeling humanity, as Self, strong for true, good, spiritual creativity…

"And when the Guardian of the Threshold wants to speak to our thinking so that it integrates itself in the Cosmos, he doesn't direct us down to the will, which should rise upward; he doesn't direct us to feeling in the wide circle in which the Sun moves; but he indicates the heights, the heavenly heights where alone the self can live selflessly if it wants to receive the powers of thought in what comes with grace from above, if it wants to follow a higher striving. We stand below, the Word is above. We must be inwardly courageous to hear the Word; for only if we courageously strive for wisdom and knowledge does the Cosmic Word resound from above, full of grace, speaking about humanity's true wisdom…

"…We must look above if our thinking wants to unite itself with the forces of the Cosmos. The realm of cosmic circling distance is where we must feel ourselves to be if our feeling wants to unite itself with the cosmic forces. Below is the place where we must look to insert our earthbound willing, which we should make free above, into the cosmic realms. Everywhere—above, in the distance and below—*everywhere is special Being*. We must feel it. The Guardian of the Threshold, on behalf of Michael, points us there and he tells us what we'll find above, in the middle and below. He instructs us further about the heights, the middle and below, because he wants to instruct us about thinking, feeling and willing..."

Lectures to the First Class, **Rudolf Steiner, Volume III, Lecture XXIII, (Recapitulation of Lesson IV), Dornach, September 13, 1924, GA 270**

"...Thus, the Guardian leads us to an inner experience of the verses, through which we can unite our corporeality with the elements to which it belongs.

"Then he [the Guardian] guides us further on to the soul. Here he doesn't point us to the elements earth, water, air, fire; here he points us to the planets. He points out to us how we should feel about what mutually draws the planets' orbits around the Earth, how one planet or another draws the orbit. The orbits have a relationship and speak to each other when the human being rises in his soul to this secret of the Universe-pointing, planetary powers. Then he lives with his soul in the spiritual kingdom of the Cosmos, just as he had previously lived with his body in the elemental kingdom. We can only psychically feel to be at one with the Cosmos if we bring ourselves to live into the kingdom of the planets and their orbits...

"The cosmic orbits of the various planets are drawn together into one cosmic orbit. We have thereby felt body and soul to be at one with the Cosmos: the body with the earthly elements, the soul with the planets.

"If we want the spirit to feel at one with the Universe, we can neither look to the elements nor to the secrets of the planets—*rather must we look to the stars*. For there is the power with which we must feel our spirit to be at one with in the distant Universe if we wish to feel ourselves to be members of this Universe in the true sense. There the Cosmos begins to intone the music of the spheres..."

Lectures to the First Class, Rudolf Steiner, Part I, Lecture V, Dornach, March 14, 1924, GA 270

"We have seen the changes which take place in a person who encounters the Guardian of the Threshold. And whether he or she is able to approach and come to an understanding of the spiritual world in any form, depends upon understanding the essence of this Guardian. In particular, we have seen how what constitutes man's inner-self—thinking, feeling, willing—undergoes a substantial transformation in the Guardian of the Threshold's domain. Especially in the last lesson here, it became clear to us how in a certain respect thinking, feeling, and willing go different ways upon entering the spiritual world, how they enter into different relationships than those which usually prevail for earthly consciousness.

"We have seen how through his will man is greatly influenced by earthly conditions. At the moment when the person approaches the spiritual world, in a certain sense thinking, feeling and willing become separated. The will, now living much more independently than previously in the soul, shows itself to be much more related to the forces which attract man to the Earth. Feeling shows itself to be related to the forces which hold man in the periphery of the Earth through which the light penetrates when it shines upon the Earth in the morning, and which disappears from sight on the opposite side in the evening. Thinking, however, is the force which relates upwards to the heavenly. So that in the moment that man stands before the Guardian of the Threshold, this Guardian draws his attention to how he belongs to the whole world: through his will the Earth, through his feeling the periphery, through his thinking the higher powers.

"But that, my dear friends, is exactly what must be made clear—*that upon entering the spiritual world a growing together with the Universe occurs.* For normal consciousness we stand here in the world while outside of us are the forces which are active in the plant, mineral, animal kingdoms, to which we have access through our senses; but which at first indicate no relationship to human beings. So here we stand, apart, looking inwards at our thinking, feeling and willing, aware that our thinking, feeling and willing are somewhat separated, apart from external nature. And we feel a deep chasm between our human nature and the expansive nature around us.

"But this chasm must be bridged. For this chasm, only the exterior aspects of which are perceived by normal consciousness, is the threshold itself. And our being able to perceive the threshold depends on our ceasing to simply accept this unconsciousness, when we look within ourselves, concerning an external nature which we perceive as being foreign to humanity. For this chasm needs to be understood as being not only extremely important for human life, but also for the entire Universe.

"Well, you see, at the moment when one enters the esoteric, a bridge over this must be built. We must, in a sense, merge with nature. We must stop saying to ourselves: Out there is nature, which has nothing to do with morality. We don't ask the minerals about morality, although it is of prime interest to us, nor do we ask the plants, or the animals—and in this materialistic age we have even ceased asking humans, because only human physicality is taken into consideration.

"And also when looking into the inner human we see what for normal consciousness is passive thinking, with which we can indeed visualize the world pictorially, but which is nevertheless powerless. Our thoughts are at first things we own which allow us to recognize the objects in the world. As thoughts they have no power. Our feeling is our inner-life. To a certain extent we are separated through it from the world. Our will does communicate external objects to us, but in so doing the external objects take on something foreign to their nature.

"Something truly great happens to a person when he becomes aware of the abyss which exists between himself and nature: *something great*. Something which has been expressed since ancient times with these words, words which must be understood anew in every age: Nature must appear as divine, and the human must be a magical being. What does it mean, that nature must be able to appear as divine?

"Nature must be able to appear as divine. The way it appears to the senses, and how reason understands it—*it is certainly not divine*. One would like to say: *divinity is hidden within nature*. It only appears to lack divinity. At the most within dreams do we see a relationship between nature and the inner-life of man. We can become aware of how an irregularity in our breathing process in one direction or the other can cause happy dreams or fearful and anxiety-filled ones. We can be aware of how the purely natural overheating of a room can give a kind of moral content to certain dreams. *For dreams pull nature into the psyche* [soul].

"However, we also know that in dreams our consciousness is submerged, and dreams are not what can directly describe the spiritual to us. Rather than the sleeping consciousness, we must see how the awakened consciousness presents nature.

"Now in nature, my dear friends, we have a relationship of the human physical body with what is solid, with what is characteristic of the *earthly* element. We have a relationship of the human etheric body with what is characteristic of *water*. However, this relationship of the human physical body with the earthly, and the relationship of the human etheric body with the liquid element lie deep beneath what people experience.

"What is closer to man is his breathing process, which is dependent upon the *air*. So it is from the breathing process upwards where the region begins where man can feel himself—*when he is approaching the spiritual*—related to nature.

"The breathing process contains the air element, in which we exist.

Air
"Above the element of air we have the quality of warmth.

Warmth
"And above the element of warmth we have the essence of light: warmth-ether, light-ether.

Light
"When we go even higher we come to a region—which we will speak about later—which does not lie so close to humans.

"That man lives and moves in the element of air is obvious from a completely exterior point of view. One needs only to look at dreams to see how dependent they are on irregularities, abnormalities in the breathing process. When the breathing process takes place while awake, we don't notice it, because in general we pay little attention to normal life processes.

"That the element of warmth is extremely essential to man is obvious to even superficial observation. If we dab our skin with an object that is colder than our body, a cold knitting needle for example, we feel the cold places that have been touched as separate even though they are very close to each other. We are very sensitive to the cold. If we touch our skin with an object that is warmer than our body, we don't feel the difference so clearly. We can hold two cold knitting needles very close to each other and feel the coldness of both. If we hold two warmed needles, the close contacts flow together at one point, and we must hold them quite far apart in order to sense them as separate. In fact we are far more sensitive to cold than to warmth. Why? We endure warmth much better then cold because we are creatures of warmth, because warmth is our own nature and we live and act in it. Cold is foreign to us and we are very sensitive to it.

"It is more difficult for normal consciousness to understand light. Today we want to approach these things esoterically. So it may be sufficient that I have indicated what air and warmth means to normal consciousness. But with this consciousness man feels air as something external, natural. He also feels warmth as something that touches him from without, and he also feels that light comes to him from outside himself.

"In the moment when a person takes the leap in his life which brings him near to the Guardian of the Threshold, he becomes aware of how intimately he is related to what otherwise seems alien to him.

"I have often pointed out how in every moment of our lives, also for normal consciousness, we can become aware of our relationship to the Universe through our relation to the air. The air is outside, the same air which is inside me a moment later, then it is again outside, the same air which was within me. But we are not aware of the fact that, in the sense that we are beings of air, that what we hold within us we let out again, then take what was external into us again, so that we become one with the whole life and being of the element of air in which we exist as earthly beings. Whereas we always carry our muscles and bones within us, so we are only conscious of their origination and passing away during the embryonic and dying stages.

"At the moment we enter the spiritual region this is no longer the case. We then feel how with every exhalation we fly out on the wings of the exhaled air into the expanse of being into which the exhaled air disperses. And how by inhaling we take into us the spiritual beings who live in the circulating air. The spiritual world flows into us when inhaling; our own being flows out into the environment upon exhaling.

"This is not only so in respect to the air; but to an even greater degree in respect to warmth. As we are one with the air environment which encircles the Earth, so are we also one with the warmth which encircles and penetrates the Earth.

"When we approach the spiritual world we truly experience the spirit entering us when inhaling, our own being streaming out into the expanse of space when exhaling, that is, we experience a spiritual interweaving of inhaling and exhaling. And we feel more intensively how with the increase of warmth—*in that we are ourselves within the element of warmth*—we become more human, and with the lessening of warmth we become less human. Thus warmth ceases to be a merely natural element; for we feel and recognize the spiritual nature of warmth—*and we feel it to be closely related to our being human.* We feel that the increase of warmth means that the spirits which are active in the element of warmth say: *We give you your humanity through the element of warmth; we take it away through the element of cold.*

"So we come to the light, in which we live and act. But we don't notice it because with normal consciousness we have no idea of the fact that the inner movements of light are contained in our own thinking, that every thought is captured light—both for the physically sighted and for the physically unsighted. Light is objective. Not only the physically sighted receive it, the physically unsighted also receive it … when they think. Because the thoughts which we hold within us, which we capture—*is light present within us.*

"We can say then, that when we approach the Guardian of the Threshold he admonishes us in the following way: "When you think, O man, your being is not in you, it is in the light. When you feel, your being is not in you, it is in the warmth. When you will, your being is not in you, it is in the air. Keep not within yourself, O man. Think not that your thinking is in your head. Think that your willing is none other than the moving, living, active air element working within.

"One must be very conscious of the fact that in the Guardian of the Threshold's presence one is divided into the universal elements, that one can no longer simply hold one's self together in the usual chaotic, dim way of normal consciousness. And that is the grand experience that initiate knowledge gives to the human being—*that he ceases to seriously think that he is enclosed within his skin*—something which is no more than a mere indication that he exists. For spiritual consciousness what is concentrated within the skin is an illusion; *for man is as great as the Universe. His thoughts are as wide as the light, his feelings are as wide as the warmth, his will is as wide as the air.*

"If a being of sufficiently developed consciousness were to descend to the Earth from another planet, he would speak to people in quite a different way than how people of the Earth address each other. He would say: The light which envelops the Earth is differentiated [The cloak of light is drawn around the air and warmth circles: yellow.] Many individually differentiated beings are in the light. One must imagine that in this Earth-light, in the light that surrounds the Earth, that weaves and waves around it, in this space many beings are present, as many as there are human beings on the Earth. They all accommodate themselves within the Earth's world of light. And for this visitor from space all human thoughts are in this cloak of light. And all feelings are in the cloak of warmth, and all willing is in the atmosphere, in the cloak of air…

"For the person who really stands before the Guardian of the Threshold this is not speculation—*but experience.* And this is what constitutes spiritual progress—*that man integrates with the surrounding world.* It is of little use to speak of these things theoretically. It is not particularly profound mystically to say that you are one with the world by merely thinking that you are, if you do not begin to experience the fact that when you are thinking you are living in the entire Earth's light, are becoming one with the Earth's light, and how by doing so, by becoming one with the light of the Earth, you go out of yourself—go out, so to speak, through all the pores of your skin into a divine-spiritual being—you become one with the essence of the Earth itself and with the other elements of the Earth's being. *This is something which must be understood in all seriousness by anyone who strives toward relationship with the spiritual world.*

"You see, light must, in a sense, have a moral effect. And we must be aware of how we are related to the light and how the light is related to us in the esoteric experience of the world. But then, at the moment when one steps over the threshold—*it becomes clear that the light is real and must wage a hard battle with the forces of darkness.* Light and darkness become real. And then something occurs to the person which makes him say to himself: If in my thinking I merge completely with the light, I will lose myself in the light. For in the moment when I merge with the light in my thinking, light-beings grasp hold of me and say: You, human, we will not let you out of the light again, we will hold you back in the light. This expresses the light-beings' will. They want to draw man to them through his thinking, make him one with the light, separate him from all the earthly forces and integrate him into the light. The light-beings who are around us are those who at every moment of existence wish to separate human beings from the Earth and integrate them with the sunlight which flows over the Earth. They live in the periphery of the Earth and say: You, human being, should not remain with your soul in your body; with the Sun's first light of dawn you yourself should shine down on the Earth, you should set with the Sun's afterglow, and encircle the Earth as light!

"These light-beings will be found enticing us ever and again. At the moment of crossing the threshold one becomes aware of these light-beings who want to pull human beings away from the Earth and try to convince him that it is not worthy of him to stay chained to the Earth by its gravity. They wish to absorb him in the Sun's radiance.

"Yes, for ordinary consciousness the Sun is shining above and we humans stand below and let the Sun shine on us; for the more developed consciousness the Sun in heaven is the great tempter who wants to unite us with its light and pull us away from the Earth—who whispers in our ear: *O man, you don't need to stay on the Earth, you can exist in the rays of the Sun, then you can illuminate the Earth and bring it happiness, so you no longer have to be illuminated and made happy on the Earth from without.*

"This is what we encounter when we meet the Guardian of the Threshold: nature, which was previously quietly outside us and made no claim on our normal consciousness, now has the force to speak to us morally. Nature appears in the Sun as a tempter. What before was quietly shining sunlight now speaks enticingly, temptingly. And we first realize that there is something spiritual living and moving in this sunlight when the enticing, the tempting beings appear in the light of the Sun who want to pull us away from the Earth. For these beings are in continuous battle with what constitutes the interior of the Earth—*darkness.*

"And if we fall into extremes—which is quite possible because the experiences in meeting the Guardian of the Threshold are most earnest and profound and gripping for the human soul—when we realize how enticing the sunlight is, caused by the light-beings, that is when we want to escape from them—*if we remember that we are supposed to be human beings.* We may not forget this. If we do, although we continue to live physically on the Earth, we are to a certain extent psychically crippled. But when we become aware of how enticing the sunlight is, we turn to the opposite side and seek relief in darkness, against which the light is continually fighting. And by swinging from light to darkness we fall into the opposite extreme. So this self, which wanted to surge out into the bright shining sunlight, is now

we think and in which we develop our soul-life, is partially putting us to death, is unmaking us.

"In the air there is a battle in which the Luciferic oxygen-spirits do battle with the Ahrimanic nitrogen-spirits. As long as one has not arrived at the Threshold, air merely consists of the chemists' abstraction: *oxygen and nitrogen*. When we arrive at the Threshold, it consists of Ahriman and Lucifer, and the oxygen is the outer mask for Lucifer, and nitrogen the outer mask for Ahriman. And a battle rages in the air. This battle is hidden from the every-day, illusory consciousness. But one enters it when the Threshold is reached.

"Once again: if one wishes to realize what exists in oxygen-spirits, what exists in the life-element when one wishes to unite his will with spiritual creativity, when one is stimulated to inner courageous activity, the danger exists that one's actions are all absorbed by spiritual acts and one ceases to be even human because what one needs as strength of will is taken over by the Luciferic spiritual world.

"And if you turn to the opposite side, then the nitrogen forces, the Ahrimanic ones that act as death in the element of air will tempt you. This is not the death which we see in the physical world; but one with which one is not personally related. If you become related to death you begin to consider it as something you wish to unite with—*and then are never released from*. Whereas in the element of life the spirits want to hold us in order for their deeds to absorb the deeds of men, on the other side—that of the Ahrimanic nitrogen-spirits—we are thrown aside into the nothingness of life. We then want to act in death, act in nothingness. We are cramped instead of being active; the self is cramped.

"Man is placed between these two opposing elements of which he must be aware with respect to his will…

Lectures to the First Class, **Rudolf Steiner, Volume III,**
Lecture XXIV, (Recapitulation of Lesson V), Dornach,
September 15, 1924, GA 270

"My dear sisters and brothers, in the description of the path of
knowledge we have reached the place where we stand before the
Guardian at the Abyss-of-being. The Guardian of the Threshold
has made clear to us that what surrounds us in the exterior world
can never reveal our own being to us; how our observation of
nature, what on and from the earth lives and moves, what shines
and speaks from the realm of the stars—to the extent we can
perceive it with the senses and with our reason—all that offers
nothing to clarify the being of our own self; that the brightness,
this glistening in the sunshine, this living and interweaving
which is so grand and powerful, so beautiful and magnificent
in the outer world, remains dark and gloomy for our true self-
knowledge.

"Then it was described how we approach the Guardian little-
by-little, who appears to us in the figure of a spiritual cloud, thus
showing us an image of ourselves; which, in turn, shows us what
we should strive for as human beings in order to achieve self-
knowledge.

"Then we reached the Guardian of the Threshold. He showed
us what the true shape of our willing, feeling and thinking is
before the countenance of the gods. He showed us how being
faint-hearted and having fear of knowledge lives in us, as hate for
knowledge, as doubt about the knowledge that is nevertheless in
us, because the character of our times has driven it into us. He
showed us the animal forms of our willing, feeling, and thinking.
It must be a shattering experience for us when the Guardian
of the Threshold awakens the forces which lead to true self-
knowledge in our souls.

"Then the Guardian of the Threshold raised us, first showing us, however, how our thinking, as we use it in normal life, is the corpse of the living-thinking which was in us before we descended to physical-sensory existence. He showed us how our body, in earthly existence, is a coffin for the deceased living-thinking—*which lies in the coffin as a corpse.* But we use this corpse for our usual abstract thinking between birth and death in order to understand the things of the physical-sensory world.

"Once we grasp how dead this thinking is, we can learn from the corpse that lies before us. We look at this corpse. We say to ourselves:—

'This corpse could never have come into being the way it is now. It is what remains of a human being whose soul and spirit were within it. The living person, the ensouled person, the spiritualized person must have existed beforehand in what lies now before us as a corpse.'

Thus, we approach the reality of our thinking when we become aware of its deadness and realize that it is the corpse of the living-thinking that was in us before we descended into physical-sensory earthly existence.

"Then the Guardian reminds us that our feeling is only half-alive, whereas our willing is fully alive—*but we are only conscious of this externally.*

"The Guardian of the Threshold also reminds us that in order to gradually find the transition to living-thinking, we should look up to the heavenly heights; that to grasp the nature of feeling we should look out to the cosmic reaches, and to gain an idea of the nature of will we should look to the world's depths, to the earthly depths.

"But at the same time the Guardian shows us how we are placed with our thinking—when we look up to the cosmic thinking in which our earthly-physical thinking is rooted—between light and darkness; how the light can be dangerous if we devote ourselves unilaterally to it, how the darkness can be dangerous if we devote ourselves unilaterally to it, how we must seek our direction and goal in the middle between light and darkness if we are to find the truth, how we stand in the middle between warmth and coldness with our feeling, and how we can vanish in the sensual embers of feeling if we surrender ourselves to the warmth, and on the other hand harden in the coldness.

"The Guardian of the Threshold indicates to us how we should walk in the middle between soul-warmth and soul-coldness on the Christ-path. The Guardian of the Threshold indicates to us that when we seek willing in the earthly depths, we find ourselves in the middle between life and death; how life would have us vanish in timidity; how death would have us cramped in nothingness—*that we must find willing in the Middle Way.* That, my dear sisters and brothers, is what the Middle Way is—as it has been described since ancient Mystery times—which the human being must tread if he wants to follow the path to the spirit.

"The Guardian of the Threshold, before whom we stand as the earnest first representative of Michael, for the real leader of this School is Michael, gives us further guidance: how we can escape from this apparent thinking, from this dead-thinking into the living essence of thinking. For this we must be prepared above all to strictly adhere to the laws which are prescribed for every esotericist in golden letters—he must only seize the gold—which the Guardian of the Threshold now repeats to us.

"He [the Guardian] makes us attentive to the yawning abyss-of-being before us, which we must fly over, because with earthly feet we cannot cross; how we will have then entered the spiritual world—*for there on the other side of the yawning abyss deep, night-cloaked darkness is still before us.* But we must enter beyond the yawning abyss-of-being into that deep, night-cloaked, cold darkness. Out of it, warmth must come to us, out of it must come light which illumines our own Self, which warms our own Self. We cannot find the firm support-point in the spirit if, whenever we are over there, we do not remember the pledge that our soul makes, now that we are in this situation, after having received the previous admonitions from the Guardian of the Threshold, who now says:—

'Do not forget that as long as you are an earthly human being, even when you have crossed over to the spiritual world—*that once you have returned you must adhere to the laws of the Earth.* When you enter the spiritual world with your thinking, you may not believe that when you return and organize your work and your thoughts in the earthly environment you may fly around dreaming within the earthly environment. You must reserve the flying for your thinking when you are in the spiritual world. You must practice deep, inner, intimate modesty, when you cross back to the world of ordinary consciousness. It is precisely by wishing to stay modest in the world, by abstaining from using the laws of the spiritual life in the ordinary world, that you will have the strength to grasp thinking in a way that it can serve you in spiritual worlds.'

"…We must go through this by letting the mantric verses [of the First Class] work on us. We must, if we wish to enter into the essential element of the earth, that means in the spiritual element of the earth; we must, my dear sisters and brothers, come to the point where we realize that our thinking is at first animal-like. We must experience fear of our own Self that is still animal-like; then the fear will give birth to its opposite and become the courage we need. That is the Guardian of the Threshold's urgently strong, earnest admonitions, which cut deeply into the heart. He admonishes us that we should feel this way when we tread the earth-element. We have already heard about treading the elements from the Guardian of the Threshold.

"He admonishes us further: when, as feeling beings, we enter the fluid element, in the world of the water-beings, that we should not be aware of fear of our own Self—*but we should be aware of how we sleep, dreaming in this water element, which is our sculptor.* And it is just when we become conscious that we live a plant-like existence in our earthly human feeling, that this feeling awakens us—*for it shows us how lame our Self is.* We will awaken once we have the humility to recognize the lameness of our Self.

"Thirdly, when we feel ourselves to be in the air element with our willing—first in the earth-element with thinking, then in the water-element with feeling, then with willing in the air-element— then we will feel in this air-element that we have nothing in willing except what our normal memory gives us: *memory-image-forms.* We must seize these image-forms, which rest passively in our thoughts, with the will—*then we are grasping the air-element in inner images.* And our own soul will appear to us as if it were ossified. If we eliminate the earth and the air in thought and imagine ourselves wanting to breathe in the air-element, how ossified will we seem. But just by feeling this death by coldness that we pass through—*the Spiritual Fire will come to us*—which we need in order to really grasp our willing.

"The verses are profound which the Guardian of the Threshold presents to our souls. Only if we observe them well and have fear of ourselves and know that we are nullified if we only perceive the Earth in thought, will we have the courage in our souls for living-thinking. When we sense how lame in feeling we are on Earth, half living and lame, will the strength grow in us which allows us to awaken, so that we are awake in spiritual life, with the feeling we had before we descended to earthly physical existence. Then, when we have willingly descended into the air-element with our memory, we feel sclerotic and shivering with cold. But it is just when we feel this shivering from the cold that the opposite happens—*the Spiritual Fire awakens*—showing us that our earthly willing is sleeping, but rooted in the living willing which was in us before we descended to earthly existence. We must learn to remember our existence before we descended to earthly existence...

"...We descend from thinking to feeling in memory when we let this verse work on us. And when we arrive at the depths of memory—where soul-life otherwise vanishes because the images of memory arise anew—there is the boundary, just as a mirror is a boundary. What comes to us from without arrives at something like a memory-wall, then it returns again and again. If one does not look behind the mirror, one does not see behind the memory-wall. But here the Guardian of the Threshold advises us that we must push through what is otherwise a boundary in order to enter the realm of spirit...

"...He draws our attention again up to the light, which however only lives in us in what seem to be thoughts. *It is light that thinks in us.* When the light pervades us, it thinks in us. But in earthly life, light is only the appearance of a thinking that thinks itself. If we don't go beyond it, untrue spiritual being will lead us to the illusion of selfhood rather than to true selfhood. So, we must realize that if we only concentrate on thinking—*we will wind up with the illusion of selfhood.* But it is just this understanding of ourselves as earthly human beings, after having gone through the delusion of selfhood—through thinking, which, however, is capable of carrying us over the abyss-of-being to grasp the world's hardships and problems—that will enable us to gradually find support for experiencing existence in thought...

"...Now the Guardian of the Threshold teaches us how in feeling, at first, we only retain the wonderful, all-embracing forms of the world. But when we only retain these forms in feeling, our spiritual experience remains powerless. Selfhood suffocates if we always only stare, feeling, at what has been formed in the world. *But if we begin to love all that is worthy in the world around us, we find being in feeling and we rescue our humanity.*"

Lectures to the First Class, Rudolf Steiner, Volume III, Lecture XXV, (Recapitulation of Lesson VI), Dornach, September 17, 1924, GA 270

"It must be clear to us that in the moment—and we have come so far in the description—when we have crossed over the abyss-of-being, past the Guardian of the Threshold, in that moment an important change takes place in the human being, that is, in ourselves.

"Let us look, my dear sisters and brothers, at our human existence as it is between birth and death on earth: we grasp the world thinking, we grasp the world feeling, we act in the world by willing. But thinking, feeling and willing are interwoven in our human earthly existence. If we want to carry out something in the near future, we consider it first, so what we carry out is already present as a seed in our thoughts. We see it flowing out in impulses of will. We feel that it is worthy. We feel love flowing to this or that being. Because we feel it, we form a thought about it. Or we go beyond that and carry out a deed of love towards the being, we let ourselves grow wings of love, and are urged forward to willing. But all that—*thinking, feeling, willing*—is closely related to our humanity as it unfolds between birth and death in the physical world. *We are at one in thinking, feeling and willing.*

"And the truth is that we are only really awake in our thoughts. They are bright and clear, although the Guardian of the Threshold had revealed them to be illusory. They are bright and clear—*we are awake in them.*

"Our feeling is darker and less clear. We are closer to existence in feeling; but the content of what we feel is like a dream—*so that we can only speak of dream-feeling, even when awake.*

"The will, however, as it emerges from our being, remains at first completely unclear to our normal consciousness. We have the thought that we want this or that; the thought appears, grasps the organism; the organism acts, carries out the thought; we see what we have carried out, again with thought. *But the will itself rests in deep sleep, as do the things in our soul rest between falling asleep and awakening.*

"But the initiate sees the thoughts in their living state; which they were in before the human being had descended from the supersensible world to the sensory one. He sees radiant being in the thoughts. *But this radiant being he sees is not the illusion of thoughts as in ordinary thinking.*

"We stand beside the Guardian of the Threshold. The abyss-of-being is there before us—*beyond the abyss, beyond the threshold*—is the black, night-cloaked gloom; but from out of the darkness gleaming, living shapes are moving. We say to ourselves—because we sense that the kind of thoughts we had as physical persons have abandoned us—we say to ourselves:—

'There is our flowing, living-thinking. It doesn't belong to us now, it belongs to the world. Light on light, thought extracts itself from the black gloom.'

"We know that thought, all our thinking, is there as the first brightness within the black gloom that we are approaching.

"And then we see something further down. We have the feeling—and the Guardian of the Threshold points to it with an admonishing gesture—*we see how the darkness below is becoming fire-like*. Fire, dark fire yes—but fire that we can sense psychically, spreads out below us. What we recognize as our willing comes towards us over the abyss-of-being. The initiate gradually learns the following:—

What happens when thinking merges with willing? The thought—of what is wanted—is grasped; then this thought merges with corporeality as *beneficent fire*. What brings the will to existence is warmth—*which is fire when our own will meets us from out of the darkness.*

"And between this warmth, from which our willing streams toward us across the abyss-of-being (for our human will is a mere reflection of our Cosmic-Will)—between this warm, dark out-streaming from below; which has at most a whiff of bluish-violet, and the bright lights of thoughts above, between both there is an interweaving, flowing warmth rising, light descending. Light-enveloped warmth rising, warmth-enveloped light streaming down: *that is our feeling.*

"It is a powerful picture which the Guardian of the Threshold draws. And now we know that when we cross over from the sensory world, from the world of physical reality in which we are between birth and death, into the world of the spirit, then we will be—in thinking, feeling and willing—no longer the unity that we are here; there we are Three. In the Universe, we are Three:—

Our thinking merges with light across the threshold; our will becomes fire; our feeling becomes light-enveloped fire.

"We must have the courage to expand and intensify the Self, the I, so that it holds the Three together when we cross over. We can do this once we are permeated with what could otherwise be a banality: that our head is the source of all our senses and thinking: All our senses and thoughts are distributed over the whole body; but what is especially expressed in our head is that in its roundness, with an opening below—*it imitates the shape of the Universe.* If we can say to ourselves in all seriousness and inner ardency: *my head is inwardly and outwardly an imitation of the world's shape.* We feel then, in that we want to view the head from within, how this perspective expands to include the Universe, which is only concentrated in our head for our earthly vision.

"We should then intensely feel how our heart, the physical expression of our soul, does not only beat because of what is in our body, because of what is enclosed within the skin; we breathe in the air, which is the impetus of the heartbeat, we breathe it out again. *The world in all its grandeur and majesty participates in our heartbeat.* What is sensed in our heart is not merely what is within us: *it is the universal pulse-beat.*

"If we consider how our limbs work through willing, it gives us the strength to not only will what is within us. Consider for a moment how the forces of heredity are in us when we are born, how the forces of karma, which we have acquired through many, many Earth-lives, live in our willing. Let us think of all that, and feel: *when we will, world-force lives in our limbs, not merely human force.*

"Just think, my dear sisters and brothers, while still here at the Guardian of the Threshold's side he points over to the brightly lit, universally living and acting thoughts; to what wells up as warmth, light-bringing, light-filled; to what spiritually wafts over us from below like warm wind—*the Universe's fire, which is the 'Ur-force' of the will…*

"…But we can do something else, recalling the Guardian of the Threshold's admonition. In this situation, as we are preparing to cross over the abyss-of-being, we must endeavor to concentrate on the force we normally use when we move a limb, when we walk or stand, when our will pervades us. We must endeavor to concentrate to the extent that we will each thought, as though it were being pushed out. We must sense the thought being pushed out as when we stretch out an arm: *thus, reality passes through the will into the thoughts.* Then the things perceived by our senses, whereas they came to us previously as the appearance of color or tone, now stream toward us from the multifaceted sensory appearance as *Cosmic-Will.*

"My dear sisters and brothers: *Learn to extend your thoughts out to the world as you learn to stretch out your hands through willing.* Just as the objects of the world respond when you extend your will to them, offering resistance, so do the spirits offer resistance when you extend your thoughts to them, in that the will permeates them. If we do this, we are interweaving reality in wisdom…

"…The next thing the Guardian of the Threshold points to is the heart, in which the rhythm of our humanity is concentrated. We cannot bring anything except feeling into the heart, that is, feeling here in the sensory world between birth and death. *But we must also bring the feelings to the heart when we are in the spiritual world.*

"If we could feel the heart as if the world were feeling our heart (because we are, after all, in the world) then our feeling would be different. Just as willing becomes the senses' multi-forming heaven-weave, so feeling becomes something which must be conceived of in a way that we can say:—

Look: Thinking, the spirit's head, becomes the will; feeling remains feeling; but rays out to thinking on one side and willing on the other. It is both at the same time.

"Therefore, at this point we must get used to concentrating on a line in which we interweave what rays upward and downward.

"This line must read as follows:—

'And feeling becomes your will's thinking, your thinking's will, the awakening seed of Cosmic-Life.'

"Then you live in the glow. This is not a dying away glow, it is the world's revelation in beauty; which can also be called 'glow' in the sense of 'gloria.' The glow here means gloria.

"…The third thing to which the Guardian of the Threshold points is the force of our limbs. The Guardian of the Threshold demands that our spirit wills our limbs, that we do not feel that what we do is the result of exerting our own force; but that we observe it as if we stepped out of our bodies and were standing beside ourselves. Then the will's thinking becomes the thinking which we unfold here: *the will's goal-oriented human striving.* And now we recognize the virtue of human diligence, what human will can accomplish in the world's evolution..."

Lectures to the First Class, **Rudolf Steiner, Volume III, Lecture XXVI, (Recapitulation of Lesson VII), Dornach, September 20, 1924, GA 270**

"...And now, my dear sisters and brothers, will be described what the human being experiences when he stands on the other side of the yawning abyss-of-being. The Guardian of the Threshold indicates to him: *Turn around and look back!* Until now you have been looking at what appeared to you as black, night-cloaked gloom, about which you had to say that it will become inner-light and will illumine your own Self. With the last admonitions—the Guardian of the Threshold says:—

'I let it become lighter, at first most gently. You feel now the first light around you. *But turn around, look back!'*

"And now, when he who has crossed over the yawning abyss-of-being and turns around and looks back, he sees himself as an earthly human being, what he is during his physical incarnation, over there in the part of his being that he has left behind and which now lies in the earthly sphere. He observes his own human-self there. He has embodied himself in spiritual being with his spirit-soul. The earthly environment is over there now. He stands there in the region, in which we first were with all our humanity, where we saw what crawls beneath and flies above, where we saw the sparkling stars, the warmth-giving Sun, where we saw what lives in the wind and weather, and where, knowing that despite all its majesty, how the Sun blazes and illumines, despite all the beauty and greatness accessible to the senses, we said to ourselves:—

'Our own humanity is not here; we must seek it on the other side of the yawning abyss-of-being, in what seems at first, to the senses, to be black, night-cloaked gloom.'

"The Guardian of the Threshold has shown, by the three beasts, what we actually are. Now will be described how in the gloom that is beginning to be light, we should begin to look back on what we as humans are in the sensory world, together with what was our only world in sensory earthly existence.

"And now the Guardian of the Threshold points directly back there to the earthly man, which we ourselves also are during earthly existence, and to which we must continually return, into which we must always penetrate when we leave the spiritual world and return to our earthly duty. For we may not become dreamers and go into raptures—*we must return completely to Earth-life.* Therefore, the Guardian of the Threshold directs us to look at the person who stands over there, who we ourselves are, in a way that at first draws our attention to what this person is. He knows that he perceives the outer world through the senses— which are mostly situated in the head, and that he perceives his thinking through the impulse of the head.

"But the Guardian of the Threshold now says:—

'Look into this head. It is like looking into a dark cell, for you do not see the creative light within it. The truth is that what you had as thinking over there in the sensory-world is mere seeming, mere images, not much more than mirror-images.'

"The Guardian of the Threshold admonishes us to be very aware of this; but also to be aware that what is only appearance in earthly thinking is the corpse of a living-thinking in which we were immersed in the soul-spiritual world before we descended to this earthly life. *There thinking lived!* Now thinking rests as dead-thinking, as seeming thinking in the coffin of our bodies. And all the thinking we use in the sensory world is dead-thinking. It was alive before we descended."

"…Therefore, we must be strong, the Guardian of the Threshold tells us, and imagine dead-thinking being cast out into the cosmic nothingness, for it is only seeming. And the willing that then arises we should consider as what comes over from previous incarnations and interweaves and works, making us thinkers. Within are the creating cosmic thoughts. These creating cosmic thoughts enable us to have human thoughts."

"…And then the Guardian of the Threshold adds—and one must strain to hear him:—

Now imagine that you are observing that figure on the other side who you yourself are.

"You turn around again and look into the darkness and try with all your inner imaginative force of remembrance—as one does when retaining a physical after-image in the eye. Try with all your strength to draw before you something like a gray outline of what you saw over there but avoid drawing anything except the outline of the figure.

"...And secondly, the Guardian of the Threshold points with a stronger gesture to what feeling is to the person over there, who we ourselves are, and he admonishes that we are to see this feeling as a dim dream. In fact, we see feeling—which makes the person over there more real than thinking, for thinking is illusion, whereas feeling is half reality—*we see the person's feeling enfold in numerous dream-pictures during the day.* We learn by observing it that—*feeling, for the spirit and in the spirit, is dreaming.*

"But what kind of dreaming is feeling? In this feeling, not only the individual dreams; but within it—*the whole surrounding world dreams.* Our thinking is our own. That's why it's illusion. *The world lives in our feeling. The world's existence is within it.*

"Now we must achieve, to the extent possible, tranquility of heart, the Guardian warns, so that we can extinguish what lives and interweaves as feeling in the dream-pictures—*just as dreams are extinguished in deep sleep.* Then we can reach the truth of feeling, and we can see human feeling interwoven with the Cosmic-Life that is present in spirit in all our surroundings. And then the real spiritual human being appears to us, who in his body lives at first in his half-existence. The human being appears to us from out of sleeping-feeling. We feel ourselves to be on the other side of the threshold, on the other side of the yawning abyss-of-being—*for feeling has fallen asleep and the Cosmic-Creative-Powers, which live in feeling, have appeared around us.*

"...The Guardian of the Threshold indicates to us that we should look back once again at the gray figure that stands over there (which we are ourselves in earthly life); but this time after having turned away—*in our minds we turn it around in a circle.* We will find, when we rotate the figure—*that the Sun appears behind it and rotates with it.* And we will realize that at the moment we are brought into physical existence from the spiritual

world—*our etheric body has been compressed from the cosmic-
ether.*

"Then the Guardian of the Threshold refers us to our will
(which is active in our limbs). And he strongly draws our
attention to the fact that—*whatever relates to the will is in a
sleeping-state, even when we are awake.* He explains how as
the thought works downward the thought carries warmth
downward into our limbs' movement so that it becomes will:
this becomes clear in spiritual-cognition and spiritual-seeing.
Normal consciousness hides this when we are sleeping, as it hides
life in general during sleep. Now we should observe the will in
the limbs as though sunken in deep-sleep. *The will is asleep. The
limbs are asleep.* We should see this as a firm mental image. Then,
when it is firm, we realize how thinking, the source of willing in
earthly man, sinks down into the limbs. Then it becomes light
in him. The will becomes bright. It wakes up. When we first see
it in its sleeping-state, we find that it wakes up when thinking
sinks downward and light from below streams upward—*which
is the force of gravity.* Feel the force of gravity in your legs and
arms when you let them relax: that is what streams upward, and
which meets with the downward streaming thinking. We observe
human will transformed into its reality and thinking appearing as
what ignites the will in man in an enchanting, magical way. *That
is the truly magical effect of thinking on the will. It is magic.* Now
we become aware of it."

Lectures to the First Class, **Rudolf Steiner, Volume II,
Rudolf Steiner, Lesson XVI, Dornach, June 28, 1924, GA 270**

"Let us imagine it once more, for we cannot recall it to our souls
too often. We see before us everything belonging to the kingdoms
of nature. We observe the glorious heavenly bodies; we see the

floating clouds; we see the wind and the waves, the thunder and lightning. We see everything from the humblest worm to the sublimest revelations in the glittering stars. Only a false asceticism, unrelated to true esotericism, could in any way despise this world that speaks to the senses. The person who wishes to be truly human can do nothing other than intimately relate to the sense-perceptible life, from the humblest creature to the majestic, divinely glittering stars.

"We must never despise the grandeur and awesome beauty of all that surrounds us, which we must acknowledge; we must go forward step by step in the world and be able to appreciate what our eyes see, what our ears hear, what the other senses perceive, what we can grasp with our reason. However, a moment comes as you look around at the expanse of space, at the interweaving of time, that despite all the grandeur and awesome beauty in your surroundings, you cannot find there what the inner nature of your being is. So you must say to yourself: the inner source of my being is to be sought elsewhere. The very power of such a thought affects us.

"What follows for the soul can only be expressed in imaginative thoughts. At first these imaginative thoughts lead us to a wide field in which everything earthly and sense-perceptible is spread out before us. We find it to be radiant with the Sun, we find it to be shining light. But as we look all around us we find our own self nowhere. Then we gaze before us and see that this sunny field, which is grandiose and beautiful and sublime to the senses, is blocked by a dark, night-bedecked wall. We see ourselves entering deeply into the darkness. We intuit that perhaps there in the darkness is our self's true origin—*but we cannot see into it.*

"And as we follow the path forward, the abyss-of-existence, the threshold to the spiritual world, appears before us. *We must cross over this abyss.* The Guardian stands there warning us that we must be mature in order to cross over the abyss; for with our thinking, feeling and willing habits which correspond to the physical sense-perceptible world, we cannot cross over the abyss of existence into the spiritual world in which our real self-originated.

"The Guardian of the Threshold is the first spiritual being we encounter. Every night we are in this spiritual world when we sleep. But it is like darkness around our I and our astral body because we can only enter this spiritual world when sufficiently mature. The Guardian of the Threshold protects us from entering immaturely. But now as we encounter him, he sends us his grand admonishments…"

Lectures to the First Class, **Rudolf Steiner, Volume II, Lesson XVII, Dornach, July 5, 1924, GA 270**

"…The human being beyond the threshold of existence, where the Guardian stands, feels himself to be within weaving, living light. Gradually it becomes not only felt light—*but a kind of light about which we can say that he sees it.*

"From feeling the light in waves, as in spiritual thoughts, so to speak, light appears which is seen by the spirit's eye.

"But the human being cannot enter already seeing into this light without hearing another deeply founded admonition from the Guardian. And this admonition refers to a powerful cosmic imagination, something tremendously majestic which the person, even while being here in the sensible world, can receive as an impression—*if he has the heart for it.* For, when he becomes magically illuminated by the cloud formations and the majestic rainbow, then he can feel as if the spirits beyond the physical sense-perceptible rainbow's glow are shining in through its colors. It is there, it builds itself up from the Universe, then disappears

conscious of it—in the dialogs of the higher hierarchies—as though the Cosmic Word itself were acting together with the higher hierarchies. And finally, we have been able to move on to the cosmic realm where the choruses of the different hierarchies resound together. Let us now bring that to mind once more— how we had already continued from hearing what the beings of the second hierarchy were saying to where the beings of the first hierarchy speak. And now we are able to hear them speaking in harmony as a chorus…

"…My dear sisters and brothers, if we wish to enter the esoteric realm, we should first feel that the ancient holy 'eyeh 'asher 'eyeh!—'I Am I.' 'I Am' is a holy word which resounds from that other worldly reality. What our fleeting thoughts understand as 'I Am' is only a reflection of it.

"We must be aware that the 'True-I Am' does not come from us in the earthly realm—*that if we wish to say 'I Am' worthily, we must first enter the realm of the Seraphim, Cherubim and Thrones.* Only there does 'I Am' sound true. Here in the earthly realm it is illusion.

"In order to experience the 'True-I Am' within us, we must hear the Cosmic-Word. So, we must listen to the Guardian of the Threshold's question: Who speaks in the Cosmic-Word? Seraphim, who wend their way through the cosmic-waves with spiritual flames of lightning—where we now stand. *The Word is flame, a flaming voice.* And in experiencing ourselves in this blazing cosmic-fire, which speaks the fire-language in the flaming fire, we experience the 'True-I Am.'

"…The cosmic Spirit-Word must speak. Thoughts stream from it. But the thoughts are creative; the thoughts are permeated with forces; the thoughts stream; and cosmic beings and cosmic events, everything which is evolves from them. In it, in the thought bearing Cosmic-Word live the word-created cosmic thoughts. It is not mere thinking, it is not mere speaking, it is force, forces streaming in the Words. Forces inscribe the thoughts into the cosmic beings, into the cosmic events...

"...The whole world, which resounds from the Cosmic-Word, which gleams from the cosmic-thoughts, is what thinks and speaks in humans, what bears the body, the thought pervaded cosmic body. The Thrones bear it, or rather the Thrones bear the thought illumined cosmic Spirit-Word that is within it...

"...In a certain sense, my sisters and brothers, it is a kind of conclusion to the path that began in the realm of illusion, of *maya*, which led us to the Guardian of the Threshold, which led us to self-knowledge, and through self-knowledge over to the spiritual realm, and allowed us to hear the choirs of the hierarchies. In a certain sense it is a conclusion when we now stand at the place where we may experience in ourselves the 'True-I am'—*'eyeh 'asher 'eyeh*.

"In this dialog we can experience, when the threefold 'It is I' streams from the heart, where it may stream from the heart; when it streams from the heart in such a way that it is the echo of what resounds in these hearts from the Seraphim, Cherubim, Thrones..."

A Theosophical View of the Guardian of the Threshold

We all move about in the spiritual world in the form of our Higher-Self—*but there we are entirely another being.* When we dwell consciously in the physical world, our lower-self is actually very much another person, a stranger to us, a being that is much more foreign to us than any other person on Earth. Abstract theosophy can simply say: *that is oneself, the other-self, the True-Ego.* But in the face of the actual reality, we won't find much meaning in the phrase: 'It *is oneself.*' And this other-self, this True-Ego, decks itself out in our weaknesses, in everything we should really forsake, but don't wish to forsake—those habits of the physical sense existence that we still hang on to when we wish to cross the threshold. And there on the threshold, we actually meet a spirit-being different from all other spiritual beings we could meet in the supersensible worlds. The other beings appear to us in coverings more appropriate to their nature than those of the Guardian of the Threshold. He arrays himself in everything that arouses in us not only anxiety and distress—*but also disgust and loathing.* For he clothes himself in our weaknesses, in things that bring us to admit:—

> Our fear of separating from him makes us shudder, or it makes
> us blush, overcome with shame, to have to look at what we are,
> at what the Guardian has wrapped himself in. While indeed
> this is a meeting with oneself—*it is more truly the meeting with
> another entity.*

To get past the Guardian of the Threshold is not at all easy. Actually, it is much easier to behold the spiritual world than it is to behold it rightly and truthfully. To catch a few impressions of the spiritual world, especially in our modern time, is not all that difficult. To enter that world, however, in such a way that we behold it in its full reality, we must be well prepared for the meeting with the Guardian, however long it delays in coming to us—*we must be patient*; for then we will experience the spiritual world correctly. Most people, or at least very many of them, get as far as the Guardian. The important point is that we should consciously come to him. Every night we stand unconsciously before the Guardian. Certainly, he is a great benefactor of mankind in not allowing himself to be seen—*for very few human beings could endure it*. To bring into consciousness what we experience every night unconsciously is to meet the Guardian of the Threshold. People usually get just to the edge of the boundary where, one can say: '*I see the Guardian standing*.' But at that moment, something very peculiar happens to the soul: *it perceives this moment in a twilight-state between consciousness and unconsciousness that will not allow it to come to full consciousness.* On that borderline, the soul has the impulse to see itself as it really is, clinging to the physical world with all its weaknesses and faults—*but this is unbearable*. Before the event can become fully conscious, the soul—through its utter loathing—deadens, as it were, its conscious awareness. Consequently—*such moments of the soul obliterating its consciousness serve as the best points of attack for the ahrimanic beings.*

We come indeed to the Guardian of the Threshold by developing a sense-of-self that is especially strong and forceful. We have to strengthen our sense-of-self if we wish to rise into the spiritual world. But in the process of strengthening our sense-of-self, we also strengthen all the tendencies, habits, weaknesses, and prejudices that are held back and limited in the external world through our education, through custom, and through outward culture. On the threshold, the luciferic impulses assert themselves strongly from within, and when the

Dweller of the Threshold, nor does he wish to do so, because he is himself that Dweller, and is in love with himself. He does not want to enter the temple and does not perhaps even know that the temple exists.

"To practice alchemy and to exercise spiritual power, one must be spiritually developed. The first step to this development is the conquering of the Dweller of the Threshold, and the key to the position is the displacement of the love of self by the love of eternal Good, which finds its expression in the Universal Brotherhood of Humanity, the fundamental principle upon which the Theosophical Society rests."

The Dweller, by James LeFevour, *Theosophy*, March 14, 2021

"The Dweller on the Threshold is considered a necessary trial for those on the path. It comes to those whose clairvoyant vision is opening up and the veil is lifted. One sees beneficent things but also, eventually, the Dweller. The Dweller on the Threshold was first introduced to the public in 1842 in Edward Bulwer-Lytton's novel *Zanoni*. In the book it is a cruel entity that embodies the sum total of all the ill will and selfish acts the person has performed throughout the incarnations he or she lived.

"In the book *Zanoni*, the dweller is described:

'All else so dark,—shrouded, veiled and larva-like. But that burning glare so intense, so livid, yet so living, had in it something that was almost human in its passion of hate and mockery,—something that served to show that the shadowy Horror was not all a spirit, but partook of matter enough, at least, to make it more deadly and fearful an enemy to material forms. As, clinging with the grasp of agony to the wall,—his hair erect, his eyeballs starting, he still gazed back upon that appalling gaze,—the image spoke to him: his soul rather than his ear comprehended the words it said. 'Thou hast entered the immeasurable region. I am the Dweller of the Threshold. What wouldst thou with me? Silent? Dost thou fear me? Am I not thy beloved? Is it not for me that thou hast rendered up the delights of thy race? Wouldst thou be wise? Mine is the wisdom of the countless ages. Kiss me, my mortal lover.' And the Horror crawled near and nearer to him; it crept to his side, its breath breathed upon his cheek! With a sharp cry he fell to the earth insensible.'

"According to Blavatsky, the 'Dweller' is a known term in occultism. The term used by students for long ages past refers to certain maleficent astral Doubles of defunct persons. In this view, the Dweller is the shell of the previous incarnation of a materialistic person discarded by the Higher Ego. Upon reincarnation, the Dweller is attracted to the soul again.

"In *The Secret Doctrine* it is explained that the Dweller occurs in such cases where the higher is separated from the lower. This happens after death when our base kamic desires and passions survive the absence of the soul's assent to the after-life. The Dweller becomes drawn to the reincarnating Ego to whom it previously belonged. It fastens on to the kama of the new personality becoming the new life's Dweller on the Threshold and giving more power to the kamic element.

"The good news is that the solution from this haunting dweller is in virtue. This is touched upon later in the book *Zanoni*. Zanoni, an adept, speaks to Glyndon, the recent initiate:

'But answer me this: when, seeking to adhere to some calm resolve of virtue, the Phantom hath stalked suddenly to thy

Further explanation can be found in what was published as
the third volume of *The Secret Doctrine*: 'The 'Dweller on the
Threshold' is found in two cases: (a) In the case of the separation
of the Triangle from the Quaternary; (b) When Kamic desires and
passions are so intense that the Kama Rupa persists in Kama Loka
beyond the Devachanic period of the Ego, and thus survives the
reincarnation of the Devachanic Entity (e.g., when reincarnation
occurs within two hundred or three hundred years). The 'Dweller'
being drawn by affinity towards the Reincarnating Ego to whom
it had belonged, and being unable to reach it, fastens on the
Kama of the new personality, and becomes the Dweller on the
Threshold, strengthening the Kamic element and thus lending it a
dangerous potency. Some become mad from this cause.

"Truly, 'The Dwellers of the Threshold' are within!" H.P.B.

John Bunyan's "Pilgrim" Meets the Guardian

The last description of the meeting with the Guardian of the Threshold that we will share is from John Bunyan's *The Pilgrim's Progress*, a religious allegory of moral training and development told as a pilgrimage from the "City of Destruction" to the "Celestial City." Essentially from Sodom and Gomorrah to New Jerusalem with accompanying *Bible* references to authenticate and sanctify what the author is depicting as moral advancement towards the goal of crossing over from the physical world into the spiritual world—a Christian religious crossing of the threshold of sorts. In this version, as the pilgrims are trying to ford the river of death, their sins weigh them down and pull them under the waters until death seems certain. To get to New Jerusalem, death must be overcome before the 'golden gate' to the spiritual world is opened. Also on the pilgrimage, many allegorical characters, named after their propensities, teach the main pilgrim, named Christian, about the shortfalls of base vices and immoral attitudes and actions. The pilgrims basically travel along a 'review of their conscience' as it encounters learning events throughout life. This review is much like what an aspirant encounters on the ascension path to the spiritual world when the three beasts show the aspirant his shortcomings and frighten the unwitting soul by the extreme amount of unconscious and unkind thoughts, words, and deeds they have done in their life. None of the sins of the world can be carried into New Jerusalem, the Celestial City.

The Pilgrim's Progress is a symbolic vision of a good man's pilgrimage through life meeting and learning about the aspects of human desire—both lower desires and higher spiritual desires. At one time, second only to the *Bible* in popularity, *The Pilgrim's Progress* is the most famous Christian allegory still in print that is applicable to current Spiritual Ascension. It was first published in the reign of the British king Charles II and was largely written while its Puritan author was imprisoned for offenses against the *Conventicle Act of 1593*. John Bunyan was imprisoned twice for his religious beliefs; which were tested to their limit by his incarceration. Bunyan's testament to faith recapitulates in symbolic form the story of his own conversion which has a life-or-death quality about this pilgrimage to the Celestial City. The pilgrim's sense of urgency is established in the first scene as Christian, in the City of Destruction, reads in his book (the *Bible*) and breaks out with his lamentable cry, "What shall I do?" It is maintained by the combatants along the pilgrimage road with giants and monsters such as Apollyon and Giant Despair, who embody spiritual terrors, just as the three beasts at the threshold confront the aspirant. The voices and demons of the Valley of the Shadow of Death are a clear picture of what every aspiring soul encounters when trying to cross the threshold between worlds.

Some of the characters, who are embodiments of parts of the pilgrim's soul, are given allegorical names, like: Talkative, Ignorance, Mr. Worldly Wiseman, the Evangelist, Mr. Legality, Civility, the Gatekeeper (the Guardian or Dweller), Good-will (Christ), and the Interpreter, to name a few. The pilgrims also travel through foreign and familiar lands, like: the Delectable Mountains, the Meadow by the River of Life, the Slough of Despond, the Village of Morality, and the Wicket-gate before coming to the River of Death. Eventually, after many travels, the pilgrim comes upon a cross and a sepulcher, and at that point his burden falls from his shoulders. Three Shining Ones then appear and give him a sealed scroll that he must present when he passes through the Wicket-gate (the threshold) to reach the Celestial City.

Christian continues on his way, and when he reaches the Hill of Difficulty, he chooses the straight and narrow path leading to the Celestial Gate of the Heavenly City. He later arrives at the palace Beautiful, where he meets the damsels Discretion, Prudence, Piety, and Charity. They give Christian armor, and he learns that a former neighbor, Faithful, is traveling ahead of him.

Christian traverses the Valley of Humiliation, where he does battle with the monster Apollyon (one of the beasts of the threshold). He then passes through the terrifying Valley of the Shadow of Death and catches up with Faithful. The two enter the town of Vanity, home of the ancient Vanity Fair, which is set up to ensnare pilgrims in route to the Celestial City. Arraigned before Lord Hate-good, Faithful is condemned to death and executed, and he is immediately taken into the Celestial City (death leads you across the threshold). Christian is returned to prison; but he later escapes, accompanied by Hopeful. Christian and Hopeful cross the plain of Ease and resist the temptation of a silver mine. The path later becomes more difficult, and at Christian's encouragement, the two travelers take an easier route through By-path Meadow. However, when they become lost and are caught in a storm, Christian realizes that he has led them astray. Trying to turn back, they stumble onto the grounds of Doubting Castle, where they are caught, imprisoned, and beaten by the Giant Despair (another beast of the threshold). At last, Christian remembers that he has a key called Promise, which he and Hopeful use to unlock the doors and escape. They reach the Delectable Mountains, just outside the Celestial City; but make the mistake of following Flatterer and must be rescued by a Shining One (guardian angel). Before they can enter the Celestial City, they must cross the River of Death as a test of faith, and then, after presenting their scrolls, Christian and Hopeful are admitted into the city.

Extract from: *The Pilgrim's Progress from This World, to That Which is to Come, Part One, Delivered Under the Similitude of a Dream,* **by John Bunyan, 1678.**

{369} HOPEFUL. I do believe, as you say, that fear tends much to men's good, and to make them right, at their beginning to go on pilgrimage.

CHRISTIAN. Without all doubt it doth, if it be right; for so says the Word, "The fear of the Lord is the beginning of wisdom." [*Prov.* 1:7, 9:10, *Job* 28:28, *Ps.* 111:10]

{370} HOPEFUL. How will you describe right fear?

CHRISTIAN. True or right fear is discovered by three things:—
1. By its rise; it is caused by saving convictions for sin.
2. It driveth the soul to lay fast hold of Christ for salvation.
3. It begetteth and continueth in the soul a great reverence of God, his Word, and ways, keeping it tender, and making it afraid to turn from them, to the right hand or to the left, to anything that may dishonor God, break its peace, grieve the Spirit, or cause the enemy to speak reproachfully.

HOPEFUL. Well said; I believe you have said the truth. Are we now almost got past the Enchanted Ground?

CHRISTIAN. Why, art thou weary of this discourse?

HOPEFUL. No, verily, but that I would know where we are.

{371} CHRISTIAN. We have not now above two miles further to go thereon. But let us return to our matter. Now the ignorant know not that such convictions as tend to put them in fear are for their good, and therefore they seek to stifle them.

12] In this country the sun shineth night and day; wherefore this was beyond the Valley of the Shadow of Death, and also out of the reach of Giant Despair, neither could they from this place so much as see Doubting Castle. Here they were within sight of the city they were going to, also here met them some of the inhabitants thereof; for in this land the Shining Ones commonly walked, because it was upon the borders of heaven. In this land also, the contract between the bride and the bridegroom was renewed; yea, here, "As the bridegroom rejoiceth over the bride, so did their God rejoice over them." [*Isa.* 62:5] Here they had no want of corn and wine; for in this place they met with abundance of what they had sought for in all their pilgrimage. [*Isa.* 62:8] Here they heard voices from out of the city, loud voices, saying, "Say ye to the daughter of Zion, Behold, thy salvation cometh! Behold, his reward is with him! Here all the inhabitants of the country called them, The holy people, The redeemed of the Lord, Sought out," etc. [*Isa.* 62:11,12]

{383} Now as they walked in this land, they had more rejoicing than in parts more remote from the kingdom to which they were bound; and drawing near to the city, they had yet a more perfect view thereof. It was built of pearls and precious stones, also the street thereof was paved with gold; so that by reason of the natural glory of the city, and the reflection of the sunbeams upon it, Christian with desire fell sick; Hopeful also had a fit or two of the same disease. Wherefore, here they lay by it a while, crying out, because of their pangs, 'If ye find my beloved, tell him that I am sick of love.'

{384} But, being a little strengthened, and better able to bear their sickness, they walked on their way, and came yet nearer and nearer, where there were orchards, vineyards, and gardens, and their gates opened into the highway. Now, as they came up to these places, behold the gardener stood in the way, to whom the Pilgrims said, Whose goodly vineyards and gardens are these? He answered, They are the King's, and are planted here for his own delight, and also for the solace of pilgrims. So the gardener led them into the vineyards, and bid them refresh themselves with the dainties. [*Deut.* 23:24] He also showed them where the King walks, and the arbors where he delights to be; and here they tarried and slept.

{385} Now I beheld in my dream that they talked more in their sleep at this time than ever they did in all their journey; and being in a muse thereabout, the gardener said even to me, Wherefore musest thou at the matter? It is the nature of the fruit of the grapes of these vineyards to go down so sweetly as to cause the lips of them that are asleep to speak.

{386} So I saw that when they awoke, they addressed themselves to go up to the city; but, as I said, the reflection of the sun upon the city (for the city was pure gold) was so extremely glorious that they could not, as yet, with open face behold it, but through an instrument made for that purpose. So I saw, that as I went on, they met two men, in raiment that shone like gold; also their faces shone as light. [*Rev.* 21:18, 2 *Cor.* 3:18]

{387} These men asked the Pilgrims whence they came; and they told them. They also asked them where they had lodged, what difficulties and dangers, what comforts and pleasures they had met on the way; and they told them. Then said the men that met them, You have but two difficulties more to meet with, and then you are in the Celestial City.

{388} Christian and his companion then asked the men to go along with them; so they told them they would. But, said they, you must obtain it by your own faith. So, I saw in my dream that they went on together, until they came in sight of the gate.

{389} Now, I further saw, that betwixt them and the gate was a river, but there was no bridge to go over: the river was very deep. At the sight of this river, the Pilgrims were much stunned; but the men that went in with them said, You must go through, or you cannot come to the gate.

{390} The Pilgrims then began to inquire if there was no other way to the gate; to which they answered, Yes; but there hath not any, save two, to wit, Enoch and Elijah, been permitted to tread that path since the foundation of the world, nor shall, until the last trumpet shall sound. [1 Cor. 15:51,52] The Pilgrims then, especially Christian, began to despond in their minds, and looked this way and that, but no way could be found by them by which they might escape the river. Then they asked the men if the waters were all of a depth. They said: No; yet they could not help them in that case; for, said they, you shall find it deeper or shallower as you believe in the King of the place. [*Rev.* 20:4-6]

{391} They then addressed themselves to the water and, entering, Christian began to sink, and crying out to his good friend Hopeful, he said, I sink in deep waters; the billows go over my head, all his waves go over me! Selah.

{392} Then said the other, Be of good cheer, my brother, I feel the bottom, and it is good. Then said Christian, Ah! my friend, the sorrows of death hath compassed me about; I shall not see the land that flows with milk and honey; and with that a great darkness and horror fell upon Christian, so that he could not see before him. Also, here he in great measure lost his senses, so that he could neither remember nor orderly talk of any of those sweet refreshments that he had met with on the way of his pilgrimage. But all the words that he spoke still tended to discover that he had horror of mind, and heart fears that he should die in that river, and never obtain entrance in at the gate. Here also, as they that stood by perceived, he was much in the troublesome thoughts of the sins that he had committed, both since and before he began to be a pilgrim. It was also observed that he was troubled with apparitions of hobgoblins and evil spirits, forever and anon he would intimate so much by words. Hopeful, therefore, here had much ado to keep his brother's head above water; yea, sometimes he would be quite gone down, and then, ere a while, he would rise up again half dead. Hopeful also would endeavor to comfort him, saying, Brother, I see the gate, and men standing by to receive us: but Christian would answer, It is you, it is you they wait for; you have been Hopeful ever since I knew you. And so have you, said he to Christian. Ah! brother! said he, surely if I was right, he would now arise to help me; but for my sins he hath brought me into the snare, and hath left me. Then said Hopeful, My brother, you have quite forgot the text, where it is said of the wicked, "There are no bands in their death, but their strength is firm. They are not in trouble as other men, neither are they plagued like other men." [*Ps.* 73:4,5] These troubles and distresses that you go through in these waters are no sign that God hath forsaken you; but are sent to try you, whether you will call to mind that which heretofore you have received of his goodness and live upon him in your distresses.

{393} Then I saw in my dream, that Christian was as in a muse a while. To whom also Hopeful added this word, Be of good cheer,

by him; yea, and when he shall pass sentence upon all the workers of iniquity, let them be angels or men, you also shall have a voice in that judgment, because they were his and your enemies. [1 *Thes.* 4:13-16, *Jude* 1:14, *Dan.* 7:9-10, 1 *Cor.* 6:2-3] Also, when he shall again return to the Celestial City, you shall go too, with sound of trumpet, and be ever with him.

{396} Now while they were thus drawing towards the gate, behold a company of the heavenly host came out to meet them; to whom it was said, by the other two Shining Ones, These are the men that have loved our Lord when they were in the world, and that have left all for his holy name; and he hath sent us to fetch them, and we have brought them thus far on their desired journey, that they may go in and look their Redeemer in the face with joy. Then the heavenly host gave a great shout, saying, "Blessed are they which are called unto the marriage supper of the Lamb." [*Rev.* 19:9] There came out also at this time to meet them, several of the King's trumpeters, clothed in white and shining raiment, who, with melodious noises, and loud, made even the heavens to echo with their sound. These trumpeters saluted Christian and his fellow with ten thousand welcomes from the world; and this they did with shouting, and sound of trumpet.

{397} This done, they compassed them round on every side; some went before, some behind, and some on the right hand, some on the left, (as it were to guard them through the upper regions), continually sounding as they went, with melodious noise, in notes on high: so that the very sight was, to them that could behold it, as if heaven itself was come down to meet them. Thus, therefore, they walked on together; and as they walked, ever and anon these trumpeters, even with joyful sound, would, by mixing their music with looks and gestures, still signify to Christian and his brother, how welcome they were into their company, and with what gladness they came to meet them; and now were these two men, as it were, in heaven, before they came at it, being swallowed up with the sight of angels, and with hearing of their melodious notes. Here also they had the city itself in view, and they thought they heard all the bells therein to ring, to welcome them thereto. But above all, the warm and joyful thoughts that they had about their own dwelling there, with such company, and that for ever and ever. Oh, by what tongue or pen can their glorious joy be expressed! And thus, they came up to the gate.

{398} Now, when they came up to the gate, there was written over it in letters of gold, "Blessed are they that do his commandments, that they may have right to the Tree of Life, and may enter in through the gates into the city." [*Rev.* 22:14]

{399} Then I saw in my dream that the Shining Men bid them call at the gate; the which, when they did, some looked from above over the gate, to wit, Enoch, Moses, and Elijah, &c., to whom it was said, These pilgrims are come from the City of Destruction, for the love that they bear to the King of this place; and then the Pilgrims gave in unto them each man his certificate, which they had received in the beginning; those, therefore, were carried in to the King, who, when he had read them, said, Where are the men? To whom it was answered, They are standing without the gate. The King then commanded to open the gate, "That the righteous nation," said he, "which keepeth the truth, may enter in." [Isa. 26:2]

{400} Now I saw in my dream that these two men went in at the gate: and lo, as they entered, they were transfigured, and they had raiment put on that shone like gold. There was also those that met them with harps and crowns and gave them to them—the harps to praise withal, and the crowns in token of honor. Then I heard in my dream that all the bells in the city rang again for joy, and that it was said unto them, "Enter ye into the joy of your Lord." I also heard the men themselves, that they sang with a loud voice, saying, "blessing and honor, and glory, and power, be unto him that sitteth upon the throne, and unto the Lamb for ever and ever." [*Rev.* 5:13]

{401} Now, just as the gates were opened to let in the men, I looked in after them, and, behold, the City shone like the sun; the streets also were paved with gold, and in them walked many men, with crowns on their heads, palm fronds in their hands, and golden harps to sing praises withal.

{402} There were also some of them that had wings, and they answered one another without intermission, saying, "Holy, holy, holy is the Lord." [*Rev.* 4:8] And after that they closed the gates of the city; which, when I had seen, I wished myself among them.

observed everywhere in life. All this would come vividly before a man's soul if he were to descend consciously into his etheric and physical bodies. And the soul's imperfection compared with the perfect structure of the sheaths would have an overwhelmingly paralyzing effect upon him if he were able to compare what is in his soul with what the wise guidance of the Universe has made of his physical and etheric bodies. He is therefore protected from descending into them consciously and is deflected, on waking, by the tapestry of the sense-world outspread around him; he cannot look into his inmost-being.

"It is the comparison of the soul with what it would perceive if it had sight of what spiritually underlies the physical and etheric bodies that would evoke the intense feeling of shame; preparation for this is made in advance through all the experiences undergone by the mystic before he becomes capable of penetrating into his inmost-being. To realize for himself the imperfection of his soul, to realize that his soul is weak, insignificant, and has still an infinitely long path to travel, is bound to arouse a feeling of humility and a yearning for perfection, and these qualities prepare him to endure the comparison with the infinitely wise structure into which he penetrates on waking. Otherwise he would be consumed by shame as if by fire.

"The mystic prepares himself by concentrating on the following thoughts:—

'When I behold what I am and compare it with what the wise guidance of the Universe has made of me, the shame I feel is like a consuming fire.'

"This feeling gives rise outwardly to the flush of shame. This feeling would intensify to such an extent as to become a scorching fire in the soul if the mystic has not the strength to say to himself:—

> 'Yes, I feel utterly paltry in comparison with what I may become; but I shall try to develop the strength that will make me capable of understanding what the wisdom of the Universe has built into my bodily nature and to make myself spiritually worthy of it.'

"The mystic is made to realize by his spiritual teacher that he must have boundless humility. It may be said to him: Look at a plant. A plant is rooted in the soil. The soil makes available to the plant a kingdom lower than itself but without which it cannot exist. The plant can bow to the mineral kingdom, saying: *'I owe my existence to this lower kingdom out of which I have grown.'* The animal too owes its existence to the plant kingdom and if it were conscious of its place in the world would in humility acknowledge its indebtedness to the lower kingdom. And man, having reached a certain height, should say: *'I could not have attained this stage had not everything below me evolved correspondingly.'*

"When a man cultivates such feelings in his soul, the realization comes to him that he has reason not only to look upwards but to look downwards with thankfulness to the kingdoms below him. *The soul is then filled with this feeling of humility and realizes how infinitely long is the path that leads towards perfection.* Such is the training for true humility.

"What has been described above cannot of course be exhausted by concepts and ideas; if that were the case the mystic would soon have mastered it. It must be *experienced,* and only one who experiences such feelings over and over again can imbue his soul with the attitude and mood necessary for the mystic.

"Then, secondly, the would-be mystic must develop another feeling which makes him capable of enduring whatever obstacles may lie in his path as he strives towards perfection. He must develop a feeling of *resignation* in respect of whatever ordeals he will have to endure in order to reach a certain stage of development. Only by proving himself victorious over pain and suffering for a long, long time can he develop the strong powers needed by his soul to overcome the inevitable sense of inferiority in face of what a wise World-Order has incorporated in the etheric and physical bodies. The soul must say to itself over and over again:—

'Whatever pain and suffering still await me, I will not waver;
for if I were willing to experience only what brings joy,
I should never develop the strength of which my soul is
actually capable.'

"Strength is developed only by overcoming obstacles, not by simply submitting to conditions as they are. Forces of soul can be steeled only when a man is ready to bear pain and suffering with *resignation*. This strength must be developed in the soul of the mystic if he is to become fit to descend into his inner being.

"Let nobody imagine that Spiritual Science demands that a man living an ordinary, everyday life shall undergo such exercises—*for they are beyond his power*. What is being described here is simply a narration of what those who voluntarily embark upon such experiences can make of the soul, that is to say, they can make the soul capable of penetrating into their own inmost-being. In the course of normal life, however, the Sentient-Body intervenes between what it is possible for the mystic to experience inwardly and what is actually experienced in the external world.

That is what protects a man from descending into his own inner-self without preparation and being consumed by a feeling of shame. In the normal course of life a man cannot experience what is thus screened from him by the Sentient-Body, for there he has already reached the frontier of the spiritual world. A spiritual investigator seeking to explore the inner nature of man must cross this frontier; he must cross the stream which diverts normal human consciousness from the inner to the outer world. This normal consciousness, while insufficiently mature, is protected from penetrating into man's inner-self—*protected from being consumed in the fire of shame*. Man cannot see the Power which protects him from this experience every morning on waking. This Power is the first spiritual Being encountered by one who is about to pass into the spiritual world. He must pass this Being who protects him from being consumed by the inner sense of shame; he must pass this Being who deflects his inward-turned gaze to the external world, to the tapestry of sense-phenomena. Normal consciousness becomes aware of the effect of this Being—*but man cannot see him*. He is the first Being who must be passed by one who desires to penetrate into the spiritual world. This spiritual Being who every morning stands before man and protects him while he is still immature from sight of his own inner-self, is called in Spiritual Science—*the Lesser Guardian of the Threshold*. The path into the spiritual world leads past this Being.

"Our consciousness has thus been directed to the frontier where we can dimly divine the existence of the Being known to the spiritual investigator as the Lesser Guardian of the Threshold. Here already is an indication that in waking life we do not see our true being at all. And if we call our own being the Microcosm, we must add that we never see the Microcosm in its pure, spiritual form; but only the part that our own being reveals in the normal state. Just as when a man looks in a mirror he sees an image, a picture, and not himself, so in waking consciousness we do not see the Microcosm itself but a reflected image of it. We see the Microcosm in its mirror image."

Esoteric Lessons III, **Rudolf Steiner, Esoteric Lesson 31, Kassel, May 9, 1914, GA 266/3**

"Verse for Saturday. My dear sisters and brothers! In ordinary day consciousness we know nothing about what's behind what we sense, imagine, think, feel and will. We are also in our dream life in this living weaving that's the background of our day-consciousness. One part of this world of which we can otherwise perceive nothing extends into our chaotic dream pictures. If we could awaken halfway out of our dreams we would experience a surging wave around us in which our soul lives from the beginning of sleep. And then if we woke up completely we would bring a memory of living, weaving dream experiences into our day-consciousness. However it's physically impossible to wake up half-way; we must go into sense consciousness completely right away. That is why we know nothing about that other world.

"*But we're really always dreaming.* This living, weaving dream world is always around us and we're in it—we just don't know it. The strange thing about dreams is that it's so easy to forget them. It's much easier to forget than anything we experience with our day-consciousness. For we cannot remember the dream again.

"Most people only think about what they experience with their day consciousness, and their dreams reflect this. It's only when one fills one's soul with ideas and feelings that go beyond daily life that one can dream about something that has its origin in the spiritual world. An individual who's immersed in their everyday consciousness knows nothing about this spirituality that's behind all of their thinking, feeling and willing. *We can become aware of this consciousness of the spiritual from yet another side.*

"A spiritual stream pours into the physical body at birth or conception as it's getting built up and gradually pulses through the whole organism.

"During the course of life there forms a new soul-seed for the next life—*which continues beyond death.* However, we know nothing of the spiritual element that streams from the previous life into physical existence with birth or conception or about the soul-seed that forms for the next life. So then, what do we actually know about?

"Our life consists of two parts: one part is from birth to the point of our earliest memory, and another part is from this moment until death.

"If one is in one's 30th year of life and remembers back to that point [of our earliest memory], one then arrives at the boundary of the in-flowing spirituality. One perceives this boundary—one becomes aware of this boundary by bumping into it. Such bumps in life remain in our recollection and form our memories. Our memories collect together—and that's our consciousness in physical life.

"Just as the seed of the new plant develops in a plant, so we work at the forces that shape our new life for the future. Good for those who have stored up good and beautiful memories. The spiritual element from the previous life that streamed in and built the new body from the time of birth on gradually dissipates during life.

"As was often said, a great memory tableau appears after death. On leaving the physical body one first arrives at this boundary where all the memories are stored up; we then see them *of it.* Why not? Because we are in the habit—the cosmic habit—of perceiving through physical senses, and we are too weak to develop a consciousness without them. What are these sense perceptions really? They also contain what we can attain from the higher consciousness: imaginations or pictures of higher reality; inspirations through which spiritual beings disclose themselves to us; and the intuitions through which we become one with the divine beings. All of this is contained in the perception—but it does not come into us. When we investigate why this is so we find that Lucifer burns it up with the fire of our passions, drives and desires. Lucifer has made his home in the heart, and that's where the burning of the imaginations, inspirations and intuitions that underlie sensory things takes place—for pictures of spiritual beings penetrate into us with every breath, with every perception. At the beginning of the Lemurian Epoch when what the Bible describes as the battle between the Elohim and Lucifer took place—*Lucifer interfered in the human heart with his fire.*

"But the heart had been created by the Elohim [Exusiai, Spirits of Form] to be something totally different. For it was created by the Elohim to be their dwelling-place. Something can be small in the physical world, and yet great in the spiritual world and vice versa. Thus the heart is only a small thing physically, and the anatomist thinks that it's still the same thing when it's taken out of the body. But in reality the heart is something that's very large or great in the spiritual world, and it was supposed to be the Elohim's dwelling-place. But when Lucifer moved into the human heart the Elohim preserved a place for themselves within it. *The Elohim can still live in it and this becomes manifest in human life as the voice of conscience.*

"Where this voice speaks something is speaking that doesn't belong to Lucifer with his consuming fire—*a direct divine inspiration still reaches the human being.* And we see that this voice of conscience became objective for men at important points in human history and stood before them. That is how it was with Moses, on whose soul the destiny of his whole tribe pressed. He climbed up Mt. Sinai; he heard the voice of his God in the burning thorn bush (that is, in the fire that Lucifer had kindled), he perceived the voice of his God, who later gave him the Ten Commandments on Mt. Sinai that became the foundation of all later human laws.

"After Lucifer had seized the human heart in this way, the Elohim had to place a counterweight on the other scale pan of the Cosmic World Order. This happened in the Atlantean Epoch when Ahriman with all the ammunition he needed was entrenched in the human brain to bring to bear his cooling effect against the luciferic fire. And the part of the fire that burns the imaginations, inspirations and intuitions of percepts that Ahriman cools down became the thoughts and ideas within the human being. (Lovelessness is a particularly good fuel for Lucifer's fire.)

"Ancient initiates always had this knowledge that Lucifer with his fire is enthroned in our heart, and that Ahriman cools this fire in the head. We find a last remnant of this is in Aristotle (who was not clairvoyant); in his statement that warmth goes out from the heart up to the head and is cooled down there.

"Now one could object that it's rather strange that both Lucifer and the Godhead live in our heart! It sounds as if there was only one heart in the world, and yet there are just as many hearts as there are human beings. We run into a riddle here—that is only one of the smallest ones an esotericist encounters, and that is:—
How did the one become many?

- Gabriel, Tyla and Douglas. *The Gospel of Sophia: Sophia Christos Initiation,* Volume 3. Our Spirit, Northville, 2016.

- Gabriel, Douglas. *The Spirit of Childhood.* Trinosophia Press, Berkley, 1993.

- Gabriel, Douglas. *The Eternal Ethers: A Theory of Everything.* Our Spirit, Northville, 2018.

- Gabriel, Douglas. *Goddess Meditations.* Trinosophia Press, Berkley, 1994.

- Gebser, Jean. *The Ever Present Origin.* Ohio University Press, 1991.

- Green, Roger Lancelyn & Heather Copley. *Tales of Ancient Egypt.* Puffin Books, New York, 1980.

- Harrison, C. G. *The Transcendental Universe; Six Lectures on Occult Science, Theosophy, and the Catholic Faith.* George Redway, London 1893.

- Harrison, C. G. *The Transcendental Universe; Six Lectures on Occult Science, Theosophy, and the Catholic Faith.* Delivered Before the Berean Society, edited with an introduction by Christopher Bamford. Lindesfarne Press, Hudson, 1993.

- Hamilton, Edith. *Mythology.* Little Brown And Co., Boston, 1942.

- Harrer, Dorothy. *Chapters from Ancient History.* Waldorf Publications, Chatham, 2016.

- Hazeltine, Alice Isabel. *Hero Tales from Many Lands.* Abingdon Press, New York, 1961.

- Heidel, Alexander. *The Babylonian Genesis: The Story of Creation.* University of Chicago Press, Chicago, 1942.

- Hiebel, Frederick. *The Gospel of Hellas*. Anthroposophic Press, New York, 1949.

- Jocelyn, Beredene. *Citizens of the Cosmos: Life's Unfolding from Conception through Death to Rebirth*. Continuum, New York, 1981.

- König, Karl. *Earth and Man*. Bio-Dynamic Literature, Wyoming, Rhode Island, 1982.

- Kovacs, Charles. *Ancient Mythologies and History*. Resource Books, Scotland, 1991.

- Kovacs, Charles. *Greek Mythology and History*. Resource Books, Scotland, 1991.

- Landscheidt, Theodor. *Sun-Earth-Man a Mesh of Cosmic Oscillations: How Planets Regulate Solar Eruptions, Geomagnetic Storms, Conditions of Life, and Economic Cycles*. Urania Trust, London, 1989.

- Laszlo, Ervin and Kingsley, Dennis L. *Dawn of the Akashic Age: New Consciousness, Quantum Resonance, and the Future of the World*. Inner Traditions, Rochester Vermont, 2013

- Plato. *The Republic*. Dover Thrift Editions, 2000.

- Sister Nivedita (Margaret E. Noble) & Coomaraswamy, Ananda K.. *Myths of the Hindus and Buddhists*. Henry Holt, New York 1914.

- Steiner, Rudolf. *Ancient Myths: Their Meaning and Connection with Evolution*. Steiner Book Center, 1971.

- Steiner, Rudolf. *Christ and the Spiritual World: The Search for the Holy Grail*. Rudolf Steiner Press, London, 1963.

- Steiner, Rudolf. *Foundations of Esotericism*. Rudolf Steiner Press, London, 1983.

- Steiner, Rudolf. *Isis Mary Sophia: Her Mission and Ours.* Steiner Books, 2003.

- Steiner, Rudolf. *Man as a Being of Sense and Perception.* Steiner Book Center, Vancouver, 1981.

- Steiner, Rudolf. *Man as Symphony of the Creative Word.* Rudolf Steiner Publishing, London, 1978.

- Steiner, Rudolf. *Occult Science.* Anthroposophic Press, NY, 1972.

- Steiner, Rudolf. *Rosicrucian Esotericism.* Anthroposophic Press, NY, 1978.

- Steiner, Rudolf. *Rosicrucian Wisdom: An Introduction.* Rudolf Steiner Press, London, 2000. GA 425

- Steiner, Rudolf. *The Bridge between Universal Spirituality and the Physical Constitution of Man.* Anthroposophic Press, NY, 1958.

- Steiner, Rudolf. *The Evolution of Consciousness.* Rudolf Steiner Press, London, 1926.

- Steiner, Rudolf. *The Goddess from Natura to the Divine Sophia.* Sophia Books, 2001.

- Steiner, Rudolf. *The Holy Grail: from the Works of Rudolf Steiner.* Compiled by Steven Roboz. Steiner Book Center, North Vancouver, 1984.

- Steiner, Rudolf. *The Influence of Spiritual Beings Upon Man.* Anthroposophic Press, NY, 1971.

- Steiner, Rudolf. *The Reappearance of Christ in the Etheric.* Anthroposophic Press, NY, 1983.

- Steiner, Rudolf. *The Risen Christ and the Etheric Christ.* Rudolf Steiner Press, London, 1969.

- Steiner, Rudolf. *The Search for the New Isis the Divine Sophia.* Mercury Press, N.Y., 1983.

- Steiner, Rudolf. *The Spiritual Hierarchies and the Physical World.* Anthroposophic Press, N.Y., 1996.

- Steiner, Rudolf. *The Tree of Life and the Tree of Knowledge.* Mercury Press, NY, 2006.

- Steiner, Rudolf. *The True Nature of the Second Coming.* Rudolf Steiner Press, London, 1971.

- Steiner, Rudolf. *Theosophy.* Anthroposophic Press. New York, 1986.

- Steiner, Rudolf. *Wonders of the World, Ordeals of the Soul, Revelations of the Spirit.* Rudolf Steiner Press, London, 1963.

- Steiner, Rudolf. *World History in Light of Anthroposophy.* Rudolf Steiner Press, London, 1977.

- Tappan, Eva March. *The Story of the Greek People.* Houghton Mifflin Co., Boston 1908.

- van Bemmelen, D. J. *Zarathustra: The First Prophet of Christ*, 2 Vols. Uitgeverij Vrij Geestesleven, The Netherlands, 1968.

- Watson, Jane Werner (Vālmīki). *Rama of the Golden Age: An Epic of India.* Garrard Pub., Champaign.

ABOUT
DR. RUDOLF STEINER

Rudolf Steiner was born on the 27th of February 1861 in Kraljevec in the former Kingdom of Hungary and now Croatia. He studied at the College of Technology in Vienna and obtained his doctorate at the University of Rostock with a dissertation on Theory of Knowledge which concluded with the sentence: "The most important problem of human thinking is this: to understand the human being as a free personality, whose very foundation is himself."

He exchanged views widely with the personalities involved in cultural life and arts of his time. However, unlike them, he experienced the spiritual realm as the other side of reality. He gained access through exploration of consciousness using the same method as the natural scientist uses for the visible world in his external research. This widened perspective enabled him to give significant impulses in many areas such as art, pedagogy, curative education, medicine, agriculture, architecture, economics, and social sciences, aiming towards the spiritual renewal of civilization.

He gave his movement the name of "Anthroposophy" (the wisdom of humanity) after separating from the German section of the Theosophical Society, where he had acted as a general secretary. He then founded the Anthroposophical Society in 1913 which formed its center with the construction of the First Goetheanum in Dornach, Switzerland. Rudolf Steiner died on 30th March 1925 in Dornach. His literary work is made up of numerous books, transcripts and approximately 6000 lectures which have for the most part been edited and published in the Complete Works Edition.

Steiner's basic books, which were previously a prerequisite to gaining access to his lectures, are: *Theosophy, The Philosophy of Freedom, How to Know Higher Worlds, Christianity as a Mystical Fact,* and *Occult Science.*

ABOUT THE AUTHOR, DR. DOUGLAS GABRIEL

Dr. Gabriel is a retired superintendent of schools and professor of education who has worked with schools and organizations throughout the world. He has authored many books ranging from teacher training manuals to philosophical/spiritual works on the nature of the divine feminine.

He was a Waldorf class teacher and administrator at the Detroit Waldorf School and taught courses at Mercy College, the University of Detroit, and Wayne State University for decades. He then became the Headmaster of a Waldorf School in Hawaii and taught at the University of Hawaii, Hilo. He was a leader in the development of charter schools in Michigan and helped found the first Waldorf School in the Detroit Public School system and the first charter Waldorf School in Michigan.

Gabriel received his first degree in religious formation at the same time as an associate degree in computer science in 1972. This odd mixture of technology and religion continued throughout his life. He was drafted into and served in the Army Security Agency (NSA) where he was a cryptologist and systems analyst in signal intelligence, earning him a degree in signal broadcasting. After military service, he entered the Catholic Church again as a Trappist monk and later as a Jesuit priest where he earned PhD's in philosophy and comparative religion, and a Doctor of Divinity. As a Jesuit priest, he came to Detroit and earned a BA in anthroposophical studies and history and a MA in school administration. Gabriel left the priesthood and became a Waldorf class teacher and administrator in Detroit and later in Hilo, Hawaii.

Douglas has been a sought-after lecturer and consultant to schools and businesses throughout the world and in 1982 he founded the Waldorf Educational Foundation that provides funding for the publication of educational books. He has raised a great deal of money for Waldorf schools and institutions that continue to develop the teachings of Dr. Rudolf Steiner. Douglas is now retired but continues to write a variety of books including a novel and a science fiction thriller. He has four children, who keep him busy and active and a wife who is always striving towards the spirit through creating an "art of life." She is the author of the Gospel of Sophia trilogy.

The Gabriels' articles, blogs, and videos can currently be found at:

OurSpirit.com
Neoanthroposphy.com
GospelofSophia.com
EternalCurriculum.com

TRANSLATOR'S
NOTE

The Rudolf Steiner quotes in this book can be found, in most cases, in their full-length and in context, through the Rudolf Steiner Archives by an Internet search of the references provided. We present the quoted selections of Steiner from a free rendered translation of the original while utilizing comparisons of numerous German to English translations that are available from a variety of publishers and other sources. In some cases, the quoted selections may be condensed and partially summarized using the same, or similar in meaning, words found in the original. Brackets are used to insert [from the author] clarifying details or anthroposophical nomenclature and spiritual scientific terms.

We chose to use GA (Gesamtausgabe – collected edition) numbers to reference Steiner's works instead of CW (Collected Works), which is often used in English editions. Some books in the series, *From the Works of Rudolf Steiner*, have consciously chosen to use a predominance of Steiner quotes to drive the presentation of the themes rather than personal remarks and commentary.

We feel that Steiner's descriptions should not be truncated but need to be translated into an easily read format for the English-speaking reader, especially for those new to Anthroposophy. We recommend that serious aspirants read the entire lecture, or chapter, from which the Steiner quotation was taken, because nothing can replace Steiner's original words or the mood in which they were delivered. The style of speaking and writing has changed dramatically over the last century and needs updating in style and presentation to translate into a useful tool for spiritual study in modern times. The series, *From the Works of Rudolf Steiner* intends to present numerous "study guides" for the beginning aspirant, and the initiate, in a format that helps support the spiritual scientific research of the reade

Made in the USA
Las Vegas, NV
22 March 2025

19952245R00193